Forever Changed

How Summer Programs and
Insight Mentoring Challenge
Adolescents and Transform Lives

Linda Mornell

TRIUMPH
BOOKS

This book is available in quantity at special discounts for your group or organization. For further information, contact:

Triumph Books LLC
814 North Franklin Street
Chicago, Illinois 60610
(312) 337-0747
www.triumphbooks.com

Printed in U.S.A.
ISBN: 978-1-62937-022-4
Design by Patricia Frey
Photos courtesy of the author unless otherwise indicated

I was born in the ghetto, a place of destruction where despair prevails. In this portion of the world, kindness was alien to me, and because of this I believed that kindness was lost. My eyes have been opened to the capabilities of the human heart.

—First Summer Search student

Contents

one   *The Beginning*   7

two   *Common Ground: Jubali*   15

three   *What Adolescents Need: Benji*   31

four   *The Interview*   45

five   *Insight Mentoring*   69

six   *Indomitable: Solaria*   91

seven   *The Seeds of Empathy: David*   111

eight   *Unfinished: Myra*   141

nine   *Discounted and Discarded: Levar*   161

ten   *Flipping the Script: Carlton*   183

eleven   *Meditation: Vasny*   207

epilogue   *No Man Is an Island* by Sasha Kovriga   229

Acknowledgments   235

| one |

The Beginning

Those who do not have the power over the story that dominates their lives, power to retell it, to rethink it, deconstruct it...and change it as times change...cannot think new thoughts.

—Salman Rushdie

It was the fall of 1989. I was sitting in my car waiting to pick up my daughter from school. San Francisco University High School, known as "University," was private and highly selective, admission a sought-after prize. We were one of the few "middle class" families. Except for the students on full scholarships, more than 80 percent of the rest were from affluent backgrounds.

As I waited, I saw a tall and very thin African American student standing by the front door. I knew his name was De'Mondre and that he was there on a scholarship because he shared some classes with my youngest daughter, who was in her senior year. As teenagers streamed by, De'Mondre looked into their faces and called out hellos. Although I couldn't hear his voice, the discomfort evident in his body and gestures was painful to watch. The students politely returned his greetings, but no one stayed to talk. He remained standing alone.

7

I immediately sympathized with his awkwardness. As a teenager growing up on a farm in Indiana, I often felt like an outsider. And it had been hard to watch my own three children lose confidence as they tried to fit into the privileged, cosmopolitan culture of this high school. We lived in a rural area called West Marin, an hour's drive and a world away from the wealthy community of Pacific Heights. Coming from a small under-resourced public grade school, they, like many of the scholarship students at University, were not as academically prepared as their more privileged peers, the majority of whom had attended private schools for most of their lives. Only years later would my kids talk about how awkward and inadequate this made them feel. At the time, I only knew they were struggling.

To help our children cope during this difficult transition, my husband and I borrowed money from his mother to send them to summer programs away from home. It began with sleep-away camps in middle school. During adolescence we found more ambitious and challenging opportunities. After their freshman year, for example, each one of them participated in a three-week mountaineering and white-water rafting trip in Oregon with Outward Bound.

Our son continued to build his confidence the following summer on a difficult wilderness expedition through the National Outdoor Leadership School (NOLS) in Wyoming. After his junior year, he participated in a community service program in the mountains of Haiti, an experience that shaped his character and values and helped him gain a much broader view of the world.

Our middle daughter was sensitive, with an artistic side. Sandwiched between two athletic and competitive siblings, she learned early on to say, "I can't," and to give in to her many fears: heights, the dark, and extending herself athletically. The idea of going on Outward Bound or any kind of wilderness program was anathema to her. We told her she had a choice: she could go voluntarily or involuntarily. She chose to go involuntarily. I still remember that angry silent drive to the airport.

She returned with a new name, "Sara Can!" The following summer she attended a highly challenging drama program at Oxford University. Today Sara Can is a working actress in Los Angeles.

Our extroverted and competitive youngest daughter found her Outward Bound experience easy. The next summer however was different. She struggled through a lonely and challenging horseback riding program with a critical coach in England.

Even with the ups and downs that all three faced, those rigorous adventures had the intended effect, which I began to call, "going for hard." By making hard choices in places where no one knew them, my children had the chance to stretch themselves and experiment with different identities. They learned to retell and then rewrite their stories, as well as to regain the confidence they had lost as a result of feeling so inadequate and academically behind in school.

I wouldn't have used these words at the time, but participating in these summer programs also increased my children's "self-efficacy." Self-efficacy is the belief in one's ability to succeed in specific situations. People with high self-efficacy—that is, those who believe they can perform well—are more likely to view difficult tasks as something to be mastered rather than something to be avoided.[1] Research also shows that people who approach challenges with what Carol Dweck calls a "growth mindset"—the belief that they can change and grow through application and experience—have much better long-term outcomes.[2]

During the physical, emotional, and intellectual explosions of the adolescent years, developing self-efficacy and a growth mindset

---

1. Bandura, Albert. "Self-efficacy: Toward a Unifying Theory of Behavioral Change." *Psychological Review.* 191–215.
2. Dweck, Carol S. Mindset: *The New Psychology of Success.* New York: Random House, 2006.

is critical for teenagers' identity formation and healthy outcomes as adults. As Albert Bandura, a Stanford psychologist who did pioneering research on self-efficacy notes, "Adolescents expand and strengthen their sense of efficacy by learning how to deal successfully with challenges."[3] Completing a lengthy wilderness expedition of three weeks or longer can make almost anyone believe they *can*— that they are, indeed, strong enough to do anything.[4]

Summer wilderness programs not only increased my children's efficacy, but they also helped them develop agency—the opportunity to act on one's behalf. They hiked six miles a day while toting a 60-pound backpack, learned to navigate using maps, and to speak up in intimate group conversations, all the while continuing to challenge themselves to master other new skills and new ideas. The choices they were constantly making mattered, the consequences of which they could see immediately. Back at school, their renewed self-efficacy and agency gave them a new sense of balance; they could see their academic deficiencies as well as possibilities with a much broader perspective.

Sitting in my worn Volkswagen on that day in front of school, watching that lonely boy, a thought began to form in my mind: *What if he had the chance to go on a summer trip?* That was the beginning, the first moment I caught a glimmer of something. The thought flew out of my head as my daughter, Mara, came bounding outside, waving and eager to get home.

Mara graduated and went on to college like her older siblings, but the image of De'Mondre returned along with the thought, *Why not a summer program for him?* A year later I started a small nonprofit organization to offer summer experiences my own children had

---

3   Bandura, Albert. *Self-efficacy: The Exercise of Control.* New York: W.H. Freeman, 1997.
4. Levine, Madeline: *The Price of Privilege: How Parental Pressure and Maternal Advantage Are Creating a Generation of Disconnected and Unhappy Kids.* New York: Harper Collins, 2006. 70–71.

found so helpful to low-income students. I decided to call it Summer Search.

For most of my life, in my different roles as student, nurse, wife, mother, and a counselor in private practice, I tended to define myself through others. Starting a program by myself in my mid-forties? Becoming vulnerable? Raising money? Reaching out to new people in new communities? All pretty alien actions for me. Surprisingly, I did those things and more. Early on there were some lucky breaks. As the daughter of a parent with a gambling addiction, I was raised to believe that nothing is permanent and that good news will always be followed by bad. When the unexpected opportunity to interview and film a prominent athlete to advocate for Summer Search came my way it was something I found hard to believe. Yet it was real.

Dave Stewart grew up in an impoverished area near the Oakland Coliseum and knew firsthand the poverty of spirit that pervaded that community. He also knew that the summer camps that got him out of that dangerous neighborhood and provided him the athletic coaching he needed had a profoundly significant impact. In 1990 he was at his peak as a star pitcher for the Oakland A's. In addition to his 100 mph pitches, he was also known for his desire to help young people escape the poverty he experienced growing up. To offer full scholarships to summer programs to low-income high school kids was right up his alley. Without hesitating, he agreed to do an introductory promo for the first Summer Search fund-raising video.

I had never been to a baseball stadium before. The dark labyrinth of stairwells at the Oakland Coliseum seemed confusing, even scary. Unsure and worried about being late, I decided to pick one randomly and began climbing upward.

At the top, there was an explosion of light as I looked down at an enormous blue-green expanse of a baseball field. There was just one person standing in the middle of that field. It was him!

A large African American man in a white uniform that shimmered in the intense afternoon sunlight, even from such a great distance, Dave radiated charisma and power that matched his fastballs.

I hurried down the long aisle between the bleachers. At the bottom was a railing. Without thinking, I climbed over it. Too late, I wondered if I had broken the rules. There was nothing else to do but to keep walking. With each step, the vast green seemed to swallow me up. I had never interviewed a celebrity before. My mouth was dry, and the questions I'd so carefully prepared flew out of my head.

Dave stood watching without moving. When I reached him, he looked down at me, squinting. "Why'd you start a program like this for kids?" he asked.

There must be something deep, something memorable to say at such a significant moment. The right words escaped me. "It seemed like a good idea," I finally said.

The squint became a frown. Dave stared at me for another timeless moment. Then, with an almost-imperceptible smile, he nodded. He turned and we walked together across the field toward the waiting cameras.

This was the beginning, the start of something that would forever change the lives of thousands of kids as well as my own.

two

Common Ground: Jabali

Just as the twig is bent the tree's inclined.

— Alexander Pope

"My name is Jabali."

"Yes, I know. The director of Summerbridge told me about you."

Dreadlocks dangled from all over his head in different directions. His smile was wide and his eyes dancing. A lively boy. On one shoulder was a large and impossibly full backpack. He wore a checkered shirt, and his jeans were worn but pressed and clean. As he sat down I caught a whiff of fabric softener. He let out a big breath and said, "So I guess you know that I am here on a scholarship?"

"Yes, I do."

There was a brief silence. It was unclear which of us was more nervous: me, a middle-aged white woman from the suburbs, or Jabali, an African American teenager who lived with his mother in a small apartment in San Francisco. I sensed his eagerness; I could already tell that he was determined to get a scholarship of some kind. He didn't know what. I had one hour to assess his strengths and weaknesses before making a decision—a challenge even for a relatively experienced interviewer and therapist. I wanted to sit quietly, but the back of my neck felt stiff and the top of the small desk was pressing against my ribcage.

Starting a nonprofit had been harder than I expected. After getting the idea, I had gone to see a lawyer. Bill Hutton, a parent of one of my son's classmates, offered a free consultation. He sat listening patiently as I explained that I wanted to give full scholarships to low-income kids, so that they could attend the kinds of summer opportunities usually available for more affluent students. The kind of opportunities that the kids at University took for granted.

"You know," I told him, "I think bringing in diversity could impact the whole field of summer experiential education as well as helping individual kids."

I was naïve, and we both knew it. Bill frowned then cleared his throat. "The first thing you will need to do is find some people to serve on the board of directors," he explained. "The next step is to find a sponsoring foundation. You could, of course, get your own nonprofit status. That would take about six months. However, since you are so inexperienced, I strongly suggest you find a sponsoring organization. They will handle the paperwork and just take 7 percent of the funds you raise."

Seven percent of nothing seemed like a lot. To my surprise I heard myself saying, "I think I'll get my own nonprofit status. It's called a 501-something, isn't it?"

Bill frowned again and his face reflected skepticism. "If you hire a lawyer it will cost $3,000." There was a brief pause. "It's called a 501(c)(3)."

I began to blush. I should have known this. The next thought: where was I going to get the money?

Oddly enough, an opportunity was right in front of me. A few years earlier, a family had moved into our little counterculture town on the coast of West Marin. They purchased 40 acres, moved into a cabin without electricity or running water, and planned on starting an organic vegetable farm. The mother from this particular family was whispered to be from one of the wealthiest families in American history—literally a Rockefeller.

She and I had daughters in the same class at the local grade school, so we were often thrown together. One day, while we were volunteering, she told me about some of the complexities—as well as the loneliness— of her background. Her parents were often unavailable due to constant travel and heavy social obligations. She used to wander around their large mansion by herself, feeling invisible. If, for example, she dropped her sweater on the floor on the way to take a shower, by the time she returned it was gone—folded perfectly and put away in a drawer.

I told her what it was like for me growing up on a small farm in Indiana. And as we become closer, I even risked telling her about my father's gambling addiction and how it affected our family. To our mutual surprise, we discovered that, in spite of our different histories, we had something in common: both of us were trying to break free from the limitations of our past.

As our girls got older and went to high school, we started running together two mornings a week. My friend often talked about her philanthropic activities and interests. As a Rockefeller, there were her extended family traditions, but she also wanted to start her own family foundation. Her particular desire was to provide seed funding for innovative solutions to persistent social problems.

With some hesitation, I explained my dream and she quickly offered an initial grant of $10,000. This woman's generosity not only covered the cost of getting the 501(c)(3), it taught me I could overcome my fears and ask people for money. This skill would be, I soon found out, critical for becoming successful in the nonprofit arena.

Once the mechanics and the funding were in place, I needed to find students. I sent out a flyer to principals in high schools from all over the Bay Area to inform them about full scholarships to summer programs. There was little response. I sent out another to guidance counselors to distribute to interested teachers. That effort brought only two responses: Georganne Ferrier, an English teacher at Oakland High School; and Lois Loufbourrow, the director of Summerbridge.

Summerbridge (now called the Breakthrough Collaborative) was an academic enrichment and tutoring program for low-income middle-school youth that used office space at University. It was actually a fruitful partnership—graduates from Summerbridge often got full-tuition scholarships to University and other private high schools across the city.

As Lois was describing some former students who might benefit from the opportunity to step out of what were usually limited environments in the summer, I looked out the window of her large, airy office. At first glance, the kids walking by seemed casually dressed. A closer look showed that they were wearing carefully chosen designer jeans and expensive looking sweaters. Many had braces on their teeth and their skin was clear—signs of affluence. Lois saw me looking and nodded. We both understood the challenges surrounding the scholarship kids at University.

Jabali's chair scraped the floor. I snapped back to attention. He was saying. "You know, at first after being accepted to University I was on top of the world. This summer I wanted to go back and teach at Summerbridge, but they said I was too immature." He hesitated, "That was a slap in the face."

He hesitated again. "So I guess that's why I'm here now talking to you."

Yes, indeed. According to Lois, Jabali had a lot of potential but was also at high risk of not fulfilling that potential at University. His first ninth-grade semester confirmed that reality. His extroverted and creative personality made him immediately known by everyone at school, but there were two Fs on his report card. The pressure to be popular—to assuage his deep insecurities and prove he belonged in this setting—combined with an inability to focus, made his first year of high school a struggle. Given those realities, Lois thought it would be best for Jabali to start early in Summer Search during the summer after ninth grade rather than after the tenth or eleventh grade.

I looked at this interesting young man now and wondered how to proceed. Lois had also told me about his poor work habits. In Summerbridge, he would complete homework assignments last minute while walking to class and skip sports practices because he wanted to hang out with friends in his neighborhood. In fact, his normal behavior was to skate by, doing the bare minimum on all academic assignments and other commitments.

Adults and even educators often label students like Jabali as lazy and undisciplined but those behaviors can also be seen as a manifestation of significant internal interference. The first label shuts kids down, locks them in; the second opens up a world of possibilities.

His feet shuffled under his desk and I noticed Jabali was wearing high-top tennis shoes. He was looking out the window as I said, "What's it like to walk in those shoes?" The following interview is recalled in Jabali's own words, his own voice:

I heard the question but I automatically said, "What did you say?"

Silence. I was sitting with this woman in the back room of the Summerbridge office. I remember there was this window. Normally I would be looking out, waving to friends, but instead there was this stillness. So quiet. I felt like I was going to get it, the scholarship to whatever; that I could charm her like everyone else. But the questions, the tone of the conversation was immediately uncomfortable. As I sat there I began to feel like I was losing something. It was like all my protection — my bravado and camouflage — was being peeled away. I wanted to stop what was happening.

"What did you say?" I asked her again.

"You tell me," she answered.

I hesitated. "Do you mean what is it like for me?" She nodded but didn't say anything. "It's hard at home."

"Okay."

"It's just my mother and me in a really small space. And, uh, she's really upset right now that I might lose my scholarship here."

"Why do you think that might happen?" she asked.

Damn. Those questions kept coming. I didn't answer right away, but that seemed okay with her.

"The kids here think I'm cool, I joke around a lot, but I'm not one of them." I hesitated and then decided to just put it out there. She could take it or leave it. "When you're poor and feel inadequate like I do here, you know, like I don't belong, well, you hide things."

She nodded like she knew what I was talking about, so I just kept going.

"It's so hard, the kids here have everything they want. The classes I struggle with seem easy for them."

"What about your father?" she asked.

"My father?" I looked out the window again, maybe hoping for someone to wave to. Instead of getting the scholarship to a camp or something, this was starting to become about my father. He had gone, vanished into thin air before I was two. I hadn't seen or heard from him since. To survive without a father, not be a fully whole person, was something I wanted to avoid thinking about.

"Some people think that a boy without a father is like an explorer without a map," she said.

That's when it hit me: *Holy shit, I don't know who I am!* It was like I thought I was a world-class boxer and expected to step into the ring and make a knockout in the first round. Instead, I was hit 10 times with quick powerful jabs. The questions kept coming. So clear and so very simple. Hearing the sound of my own voice, I wondered why I was stumbling. I could feel my face starting to get hot.

"I never asked my mother about him because they didn't get married. I don't want to make her feel bad because she works really hard to support us. She's a mail carrier."

"What about race? How does it play out?" she asked.

"My dad is black and my mom white," I was starting to feel sort of irritated. "What do you mean about it 'playing out.'"

She paused for a few seconds and said, "I guess what I'm asking is how does race impact you here at University."

"That's just it—it doesn't, except for the fact that I don't fit in anywhere. That's why I wanted to teach at Summerbridge this summer, you know be a role model for my kind of kids who don't have anyone."

Then she said, "This is just a guess right now, Jabuli, but I get the sense that you care a great deal about how other people feel—your mother, your friends, the middle-school kids at Summerbridge. I find that impressive. I think you will benefit from becoming a Summer Search student."

I left that interview feeling weird. Just before it ended, I think she said, "You are not all there yet. But you can be and you will do great things." Over the years I have often wondered, did she really say that?

For an adolescent, to be poor in the middle of great affluence and academically unprepared at rigorous private school is to *suffer*. I could see why Summerbridge staff felt he was not yet ready to become a teacher. He was easily distracted, which made our interview challenging—he kept changing the subject and asking me to repeat questions before finally settling down and turning his full attention to me and to what he was saying. To make up for those insecurities at University, Jabali tried to be "cool." He wanted everyone to like him, and they did, but the cost was high. Needing to constantly respond to and joke around with his peers limited his ability to focus on academics. It was also clear that he had a tendency to cut corners, fake it. We were almost at the end of his interview before he finally admitted that he had failed two classes.

It was taking a lot of Jabali's energy to hide parts of himself. Yet, when given this opportunity to speak honestly, he found the courage to start the process of coming out of hiding.

Jabali did indeed charm me, and I certainly had a scholarship for him. But to what program? An organization called Chewonki ran an amazing seven-week boat-building program in Maine for boys. That year they had one empty spot which they offered to Summer Search at a substantial discount. For the first three weeks, the boys build their own kayaks with two master carpenters, and over the next few weeks, they go on a wilderness expedition—using those very boats. An extraordinary opportunity, especially for a boy without a father.

When I told him about the program, Jabali wasn't sure he wanted to do anything longer than three weeks. Yet I felt it was essential that he "go for hard," so I was unwilling to negotiate. Finally, he said okay.

And so this talented and distracted boy chose to take on the greatest challenge of his life. He told me later, "At Chewonki I sort of felt like a little kid following his grandpa around in the basement picking up tools. Then I got this manly sense from the incredible triumph of building something with my own hands. For the next month we went from island to island being exposed to the elements after paddling 20 miles a day amidst *four- to eight-foot swells*. When I came back to school where everyone had more money and cooler clothes, I was the only one who had that experience. I had done something that demanded their respect."

Jabali gained my respect too.

The year before, after the first group of fourteen Summer Search students completed their trips, I learned that when they got home there was a serious dip in morale. Returning home, triumphant, only to be faced with the same hard challenges in their lives and with people who couldn't grasp the meaning or magnitude of their success often triggered a depression. Writing a post-trip essay helped—when important experiences are committed to writing, they stick around longer—but it wasn't enough.

I decided to address that problem by organizing a public event for participants, their parents, and referring teachers—the chance for everyone to come together and celebrate their big risks and successes. I also wanted to build community.

That second year, 1991, we held the Fall Event at St. Elizabeth's, a Catholic school in East Oakland. As the evening got underway, I noticed that Jabali was missing. This confirmed something I worried about. Maybe, just maybe, underneath his showy personality and bravado, he was a kid who couldn't be trusted to follow through. Maybe dealing with the feelings that caused his internal interference was something too hard, something he needed to avoid. Or, more simply, maybe his tendency to cut corners was too entrenched.

Then I saw him slip in the back door with his mother, Vicki. After the program ended, I talked with them both and learned that Jabali, with a temperature of 102, had been too sick to go to school that day. In fact, he was too sick to even sit up in the car, and had made the journey to Oakland lying down on the back seat. I looked at his pallid and sweating face and realized that it was okay. This boy had character—and his mother understood the importance of giving back. I didn't have to worry. I could count on them. *There was common ground.*

From that moment on, I gave Jabali my full support and allegiance as we worked together throughout high school to develop his strengths. There would be two more trips coming over the next two summers as well as frequent check-ins with me at the Summer Search office.

That fall, as I walked into University for an appointment with Lois, I crossed through the large hallway that led into an outdoor courtyard. Everywhere, samples of some of the students' summer experiences were on display: excellent photos documenting a trip to France, more pictures of community service in Ghana. Some stunning artwork from a summer program at Northwestern University. Then it hit me, what about Jabali's boat? How about getting Jabali's kayak back from Maine? We could put it right here in the middle of this courtyard. Yes, right in the middle of this private school!

I went to see the headmaster. Peter Estey was taken aback by the idea. "How large is it?" he asked.

"Well, you're going to have to rent a truck," I said. "In talking to Chewonki, they think the cheapest way to get it here is to ship it by train. Summer Search will pay for it but you will need to pick it up in Oakland."

For the next six months, Jabali's beautiful kayak was displayed in that courtyard, a perfect symbol of his achievement. Now, 22 years later, it is safely stored in a friend's garage, a cradle for stray cats and an ongoing reminder of the courage of that first huge step out.

Things started to change for Jabali in his sophomore year as he began to realize that there was a way to articulate things, to talk about what hurt him the most. As he began talking more directly about his feelings, including his feelings of confusion and loss about not having a father, his "internal interference" lessened and his ability to focus in school improved. Better grades allowed him to play soccer and basketball, sports he loved. School life became more stable as well as more bearable. Although he still had a long way to go, he was no longer at such high risk academically.

The following summer, Jabali agreed to attend another wilderness expedition, and I immediately thought of NOLS, the summer program my own son had done when he was at University. Jabali was attracted by a shorter program in Wyoming, but I felt again that the bigger the challenge the better, and pushed him to go on a NOLS trip in Alaska.

"I spent a month in the Talkeetna Mountain Range about 100 miles out of Anchorage," Jabali wrote in his essay when he returned home. "It was the most profound, pristine experience I have ever had with nature at its most basic elements."

In his junior year, Jabali returned to school with even greater self-confidence, and his grades continued to improve. He made the varsity basketball and soccer teams. And he picked up some provocative language. His soccer coach at University was from Ghana and had this made-up word, "boder." Boder meant "great," and he would shout out "Boder!" every time they made a goal. Jabali loved that word so took it on as his own and began ending most conversations with boder, you know, just to shake people up.

In January of that year, we met again at school to review his progress as well as to talk about the coming summer. In addition to getting the grades to play sports, school was easier. Jabali's tendency to kid around and entertain his classmates was coming from a less pressured place. No longer marred in deficit, his creativity and unique spirit was emerging. In fact, he was nominated by his school for a new TV show created by NBC called *Straight Talk 'N Teens*. He auditioned and got the role of host. The show dealt with teen issues like drugs, racism, body image, as well as teen culture (fashion, music, media, etc.). Jabali brought an energy and honesty to his role and became pretty popular. He told me he was starting to get fan mail.

Did he need another trip? Probably not, yet it felt like we were not quite done. He had taken a leap of faith and done two incredibly difficult trips. Maybe his next trip, his last trip, should be something out of the country. As we talked, a memory from my own childhood surfaced:

I was about 10 when my parents took me and my sisters to our grandmother's house. They were off to Mexico on vacation. It was rare for my family to leave us or Indiana, and they had never left the country, so this trip seemed incredibly exciting, even glamorous. For Rex and Louise, it was their first big step out.

The first stop was in the border town of Tijuana. Dad parked the car, and they prepared to set off to explore the town. However, as soon as they stepped a few feet away, two Mexican policemen emerged from the shadows and wiped a thick layer of dust off a small section of the curb. Red. This was a parking violation, and the policemen demanded a fee. My father was a stubborn man and not much of an abstract thinker, so he pointed to the remaining curb that was covered with dust and refused. The ensuing argument quickly escalated, but Daddy wouldn't give in. The policemen finally hauled him off to the local jail.

Mother, on her dream-of-a-lifetime trip, sat waiting in the stifling heat while Daddy fumed in his cell. After several hours, he reluctantly paid the bribe. When they released him, he grabbed her, and they headed straight back to Indiana.

During the long summer evenings, it was too hot to stay in the house. As we sat outside watching fireflies, this story was endlessly repeated. We listened closely. Each time there was a slightly different version, yet the conclusion was always the same. Daddy's voice, smug with the satisfaction of a man who has had his prejudices confirmed, echoing, "Girls, remember, you don't ever want to leave this country."

Common ground. Jabali was looking at me eagerly. I said, "What do you think about a service trip to Samoa?" He began to tear up.

How many moments do any of us have in a lifetime that can match the joy of one like this?

A few months later, Jabali was off to Samoa with World Horizons, a community service program that needed another boy. The program director was delighted with Jabali and offered a significant scholarship.

The afternoon he returned home, he called in right away, saying, "The first two summer trips were about me. You know, pushing myself beyond what I dreamed was possible helped me break the limited thinking and artificial boundaries that threatened to choke me. Those trips changed me forever, but this summer in Samoa was not about me. It was about something else. This time, Linda, it was about community and the importance of helping others."

In his required essay, Jabali wrote about the new lessons he had absorbed:

> After my trip, I realized that a lot can be learned about a country or a community by their public transportation system. In Samoa, nobody ever stands on a bus, even when the small wooden buses become crowded and there are no remaining empty seats. Instead, when a person needs a seat, they simply sit on someone's lap. As the bus fills up more laps become seats. When it's packed during rush hour, you can have three people in one seat all sitting on laps. I thought to myself, *Man, that would never happen on MUNI in San Francisco.*
>
> Samoa taught me that it's not what you have, but what you have to offer. The houses there are thatched-roof huts called *fales*. A fale is essentially a floor and a roof with no walls. I asked Malai, a young woman in town who took us on and treated us like brothers and sisters, why the houses have no walls, and her response rocked me to the core. "They have no walls because it lets people know that our homes are open and welcoming to everyone in all four directions. That is the Samoan way." I can't say that is my way yet, but I sure want it to be.

Twenty-two years later, Jabali Sawicki called the office and left a message for me to be sure and catch him on *60 Minutes* on Sunday night. On his journey toward what he heard from our initial interview about "not being all there yet" to "becoming great," this is how he described what he did:

> If it wasn't for the boosts of the trips and the chance to talk about my feelings, I truly believe I would have lost what little confidence I had. In the ninth grade, my academics kept slipping and I could feel myself getting angry. Had it not been for Summer Search, I might have squandered those resources and opportunities and probably would have dropped out and gone to a public high school. And now, as I know all too well, when there are negative shifts for African American boys, like so many of my brothers...the descent is rapid.
>
> Don't get me wrong. I would have graduated from high school and gone to some college — I just never would have gone "beyond." I guess what I mean is, beyond my limitations and fears.
>
> Although I was in two other wonderful programs, Summerbridge and A Better Chance, it was Summer Search that created the different outcome. Back at school for eight months, I would say to myself, "I can do this." And after every summer I came back not feeling down but feeling, "Man, I can do this. Man, I love life. Man! I've been to the mountain top!"
>
> Graduating from University, I got a significant scholarship to Oberlin College in Ohio. I was there for five years, which included a study abroad year to Zanzibar to learn about coastal ecology. Once you open yourself to the world, you become hungry for more. Each summer I returned to lead high school students to do community service with World Horizons, the program I attended the summer after my junior year. I went with the first group back to Samoa, then Puerto Rico, and finally Nevis. You see, I was taking the time, using the resources available to slowly fill in the gaps.
>
> Returning to my dream to be a teacher, I taught science for middle-school students at Roxbury Prep, the top performing charter school in the state of Massachusetts. Then I spent one year in New York to get my master's degree in education at Columbia Teachers College.
>
> In 2004, after a year of planning, I opened Excellence Boys Charter School in Brooklyn's Bedford Stuyvesant neighborhood. It was a K-8 that served 100 percent boys

of color. My commitment was to stay eight years until the first class graduated, which I did. This was a defining experience for me—a chance to create a nurturing place for boys, a place where they could succeed—and they do. In our fourth year of operation, Excellence was ranked the highest performing public elementary school in New York City.

Our real challenge was to create an environment where students never feel the need to be anything but their true selves. A safe place where school was cool, where scholarship was to be celebrated, and where students were a part of a brotherhood. A quiet place where, instead of projecting a false sense of self, kids could take pride and strength in presenting their authentic selves to the world.

We accomplished this by striking the right balance of joy and rigor, holding our scholars to incredibly high academic and behavioral expectations, and by demanding excellence from every member of the school community. I also worked 18 hours a day.

As an educator it is essential to identify and nurture the infinite potential of each child. *"You are not all there yet. But you can be and you will do great things."* So many of our children are written off because of their color, their financial situation, or their zip code. But when given the opportunity to shine, to grow, to be challenged, and to overcome

those challenges, our children do rise to the occasion. It was a long road for me and a long road for many of my students, but when you have adults believing in you and helping you navigate the pitfalls along the way, well, that's when great things happen.

But as wonderful as this intervention was and continues to be, even at full capacity our school only serves 600 students, a drop in the bucket when you consider the millions of young men of color our schools are failing.

Today, I am with a group of other highly talented and committed educators who have created a nonprofit called ZEARN. We're building rigorous digital math lessons for third-through eighth-grade students. I will be the online math teacher for thousands of students all over the country.

I have also become the father I never had and always longed to be. My son is two years old, and his name is Jameo Justice. He is not all there yet. But he can be and *he will do great things.*

Boder!

| three |

What Adolescents Need: Benji

Can it be that by protecting our kids from unhappiness as children, we're depriving them of happiness as adults?

—Lori Gottlieb

After my children started school, and during the years they participated in summer programs, I shared a private counseling practice with my husband. Seeing how powerful these programs could be during the vulnerable adolescent years, I came to think of them as "emotionally corrective experiences." So I dedicated part of my practice toward counseling families about how to choose the best summer opportunities for their children. I became known for helping adolescents who were reluctant to leave home make the leap to participate in some kind of program—most often a wilderness expedition.

Once I started Summer Search I decided, with some regret, to close my private practice and focus solely on nonprofit work. Occasionally,

I continued to volunteer to help families with adolescents who were struggling and who would benefit from those "emotionally corrective experiences." Although the process was often bumpy the results were overwhelmingly positive and the work was rewarding. One family in particular I will always remember.

This family was well known and well respected in the San Francisco philanthropic community. They supported many charities, including Glide Memorial Church's program to feed the homeless, Planned Parenthood, and the San Francisco Jewish Community Federation. When I heard they were struggling with one of their children, I was eager to help.

The oldest son, a young man by the name of Benji, called to make the appointment. Before we hung up, he offered—lobbied, actually—"My parents think I should go camping this summer. It's important for you to know that I hate camping."

Oh boy, I thought as I hung up the phone…this is going to be a challenge.

In her book *The Price of Privilege*, Madeline Levine writes, "The danger of the culture of affluence is the ways in which it interferes with the development of a sense of self. It is hard to develop an authentic sense of self when there is constant pressure to adopt a socially facile, highly competitive, performance-oriented, unblemished self."[1] In that environment, no one ever quite measures up. Levine also cites data suggesting that an alarming 30 to 40 percent of teenagers from affluent homes experience distressing psychological symptoms like depression and anxiety.[2]

According to the psychologist Erick Erickson, author of *Childhood and Society*, the most important developmental task during adolescence

---

1. Levine, Madeline: *The Price of Privilege: How Parental Pressure and Maternal Advantage Are Creating a Generation of Disconnected and Unhappy Kids.* New York: Harper Collins, 2006. 65.
2. Levine, Madeline: *The Price of Privilege.*

is for young people to create an internalized sense of their own unique identity. If they fail in this task, they risk *identity crisis and role confusion:*[3] an uneasy feeling that underneath the grades and achievements, as well as the struggles, lies an uncomfortable emptiness.

I had discovered that summer programs—especially those that revolve around wilderness expeditions—could be the opportunity for teens to find that internalized sense of self. Separating from home (and their parents' voices) to focus inward, while at the same time learning to depend on a group of peers, experimenting by taking positive but never the less actual risk, and finding joy in nature could go a long way toward filling that internal vacuum, as it did with my own children. But what would it do for a young man who hated camping?

Economics, of course, plays a huge role in terms of kids having access to these kinds of experiences. They are expensive. Affluent youth have the economic ability to participate, yet often today's parents are reluctant to let them separate for any length of time, especially if there is any hint of risk involved. Affluent parents also tend to focus on programs and activities that promote competitive skills—like academics or sports. They sometimes believe those qualities are more attractive to colleges than programs that focus on finding internal motivation through living in the moment and "going for hard."

Many parents feel that the best antidote for adolescent angst is a challenging, time-consuming summer job. Yet some studies show that the benefits of working for adolescents have been overestimated, while the costs have been underestimated. For example, disposable income can increase immediate gratification, promote new heights of consumerism, increase alcohol and drug use, and eclipse extracurricular activities that are important to healthy adolescent development. Psychologist Laurence Steinberg studied the effects of

---

3.   Erikson, Erik H. "Eight Stages of Man." In *Childhood and Society,* 2nd ed. New York: Norton, 1964. 261–263.

part-time teenage employment and found that teenagers who worked more than 20 hours per week reported less engagement in school, more modest education aspirations, increased drug and alcohol use, more cheating and cutting class, and lower grades. Sixty percent of teenagers spend all the earnings on personal needs.[4]

A knock on the door interrupted my thoughts. It was Benji and his parents. We sat down together, and it was clear in the first few minutes that this was a family in crisis. Benji, in his third year in a private high school in San Francisco, had been arrested for trying to buy beer on a recent trip with his baseball team and temporarily suspended from school. There were other worries too. His grades had slipped during the all-important junior year, and he was even losing interest in his one passion: baseball. His parents, Don and Janie, had put him on tight restrictions—no driving, and no socializing after school. To use an old-fashioned word, he was grounded.

It was now late spring. Summer was looming: what were they going to do?

When families come in with a problem, I first meet with the student alone and then speak separately with the parent or parents. Finally, we sit down together to discuss a plan.

I listened as Benji, a handsome, muscular boy in fashionably torn jeans and an expensive looking shirt, talked freely about the pressures he was feeling in school and at home. As he spoke, his freckled face was rigid with unhappiness. He sounded belligerent as he said, "All my parents care about are my grades. Yeah, it's true they slipped and, yeah, it's my junior year. But that's no problem. School has always been easy for me. I'll make it up. Right now, I want to stay home with my friends for the summer. If my parents get off my back, I

---

4. Steinberg, Laurence B, Bradford Brown, and Sanford M. Dornbusch. "All Work and No Play Makes Jack a Dumb Boy." In Beyond the Classroom: Why School Reform Has failed and What Parents Need to Do. New York: Simon and Shuster. 1996. 163–182.

might get some kind of job. They don't really care, they just want me to not cause any more problems so they can go to Tahoe."

Like many adolescents, this young man was resentful of authority and determined to make his own choices. I considered what a summer job might do for him. Sure, it would provide structure and discipline—but what else? The money he would make would surely go toward his consumer needs. But Benji had moved on to complaining more about his parents. "So I just had a beer in my back pocket. What's the big deal? They think I should go camping. I told you already that I hate camping. Why would anyone ever go camping?"

After several years of listening to kids who were facing much bigger problems, it took me a few minutes to sympathize with the angst that fueled Benji's entitled attitude. Yet the longer I listened, the more compassion I felt. This boy was clearly a pain in the ass, but from our brief interaction, I also got the impression that he felt he was only valued for how he performed in school.

I spoke to his parents next, while Benji waited outside the office. They were a handsome couple in their mid-forties, fit and tanned; still, I could see the stress on their faces. Don had worry lines on his forehead, and Janie's mouth was hard and set. Initially, they were tense; but soon their rigid expressions began to soften as they vented their frustrations and described Benji's out of control behaviors. Not only was he suspended from school, at home he was rude, sullen, and uncommunicative.

"He just doesn't care about anything," Janie said. "He already has everything he wants, so we can't threaten to not buy anything that matters to him."

Don added in a raised voice, "He says that we can't tell him anything, he has to experience it for himself—"

"Yeah," Janie added, interrupting her husband, "he's always been that way. He doesn't like to lie, so he waited to smoke pot until this year, you know, after he turned 16, so he could tell us about it."

Don frowned. "Maybe we have been too easy—"

"I've told you that for years," Janie interrupted again.

Don looked at her briefly, his face expressionless. Then he turned to me and said, "He's a great baseball player with a natural ability but no discipline."

I wondered what turning 16 had to do with it being okay to smoke pot. Then I remembered that's what we told our kids too. Wait to try it, we said. But if they wanted to experiment, tell us first. Of course, we didn't really mean it.

Before I could reply, Janie said, "We grounded him for six months, and all of our peers—you know all the other parents—were horrified. Even his girlfriend called me to complain."

She sighed. "I am so relieved. This has been so hard, I'm glad that someone else is going step in and to tell us what to do, someone with more power than he has."

As I listened to Don and Janie, I understood why they wanted him to have a structured experience away from home. They were worn out and certainly needed a break from the constant power struggles. At the same time, it sounded like they were afraid of Benji's tendency toward explosive outbursts. Their anxiety made the problems worse. They were too careful and had begun to tiptoe around their son, which reinforced his impression that he was in charge. Like many parents of angry adolescents, they wanted to avoid confrontations.

It was time for us all to sit down together. As I opened the door and invited Benji to join us, I heard a snatch of music coming from a passing car. I took a deep breath as I felt the tension in the room escalate. My heart was beating faster. Benji was in control of his entire family. That had to stop. *Go for hard*, I thought to myself.

Don't equivocate—he will only take advantage of any potential openings later.

I began to explain to the three of them that a decision had been made. Benji was going to some kind of program, but he could choose which one. Looking at Benji, I said, "You are too old for camp; camps are for middle-school students. What you need is a program where you can step away from the pressures in your life and find out who you are. That means a month-long wilderness expedition." The tension seemed to fill the room, so I tried to soften my stance, saying, "If you agree to go willingly, Benji, the trade-off will be that you can have more free time to spend with your friends when you return." Instead of returning my gaze, Benji was looking somewhere over my shoulder. A red flush was starting to creep up his neck.

I glanced at Don and Janie. Their faces were blank. "You have a choice," I emphasized, keeping my voice even and calm as I looked again at Benji. "As a first step, I want you to look at three very different opportunities: Deer Hill in Colorado, a mountaineering and service organization; Voyager Outward Bound in Minnesota, for canoeing; and a very special kayaking wilderness challenge with a program called Chewonki in Maine." More silence.

Benji jumped up, shaking. His whole body was rigid and his fists were clenched. He was a big kid and strong. For a moment, I wondered if he was going a punch a hole in the wall of my office. Instead, he began to cry. Tears streaming down his face, he turned to his parents and said, "Don't make me go, I want to be home this summer. My friends are counting on me. I'll get a job, I'll do whatever you want." When Don and Janie didn't respond, he grabbed Janie's hand. "Mom, you know how I'll hate this, it's not for me. I promise I'll do anything you want, just please, please don't make me do this."

Janie and Don looked at each other but didn't speak. I held my breath. So many parents are unable to tolerate, let alone absorb, then shoulder, the unhappiness of their children. Slowly, still looking at each other, they nodded. Then Don turned to his distressed son and said, "Your mom and I are going to stick with this plan."

There was a pause. "I know this is hard, Benji," I said. "We all know this is not what you had in mind for the summer. But remember you have three very good choices."

He turned to me, freckles popping on his now bright red face. "Yeah. I'm fucked, and I'm fucked." His voice rising, "And *I'm fucked!*"

"I guess you could say that's true," I said.

Later that night, the words of Kurt Hahn, the founder of Outward Bound, a program that since 1941 has challenged and shaped the characters of thousands of kids—including my own— drifted through my mind: *From successful experience in an elemental setting, one can learn better to respect self. From respect of self can flow compassion and concern for others.*[5]

How was a boy like Benji going to understand those words and get those values, unless forced to step out of his narrow—and very comfortable—comfort zone? How was he going to develop empathy? Given the stresses of the intervention, I felt great respect for Janie and Don. Character matters, and hopefully, with their help, Benji was going to find some this summer.

So what happens when a youngster is forced to attend a summer program when he doesn't agree with or understand the purpose of it? Though I'd only just met Benji, I sensed that most of his actions were, in fact, reactions. Underneath his unhappiness and anger, he did not seem to have a strong sense of who he was—only a deep-seated resentment for what he thought others expected him to be. To my mind, he lacked internal motivation. Researchers might

---

5. Source for Kurt Hahn quote, *Outward Bound Instructors Manual.*

call this a mastery orientation to learning, which is the quality that propels youngsters to care about increasing their competence over time regardless of rewards or grades or the perception of others.[6] It is internal motivation that sustains adolescents as they engage in the lengthy process of experimentation to discover, and then slowly fine-tune, their own authentic selves.

Benji, at least according to his parents, "just didn't care about anything."

After our meeting, Benji pressed both Don and Janie, one after the other, to change their minds. When he finally realized that he was no longer calling the shots, he seemed to relax and was even a bit easier to live with. When the time came, he still went kicking and screaming (just like my middle daughter) to the program he had chosen: Deer Hill.

All three programs would have been excellent, but Deer Hill would have been my first choice for Benji too. Doug Capelin, the founder

6. Dweck, Carol S. and Ellen L. Leggett. "A Social-cognitive Approach to Motivation and Personality." *Psychological Review.* 256–73.

of Deer Hill, was specifically interested in character development. Participants were expected to take risks and responsibility for their words and actions and then practice what they had learned. I was hopeful that the underlying values driving the program would penetrate Benji's defenses and force him to take a clear look at himself, instead of blaming others as the source for his unhappiness. The combination of wilderness and service might also help Benji become more aware of the worlds that existed outside his affluent home and privileged private school.

As usual, there was no word from Benji during his trip, a reality that most parents—including me and in this case Don and Janie—found unnerving. Doug emailed me just before Benji returned home that he came to camp with a resentful attitude, but that, after a few difficult conversations, things had finally worked out. Most importantly, Benji didn't quit and successfully completed his challenging trip.

When Benji arrived home, he didn't want to talk to me. This, too, was not unusual. I did follow up with a phone call to Don and Janie, who reported that he seemed calmer and happier.

Years later, while researching the effects of summer programs on character development in adolescents, I sent Benji an email hoping to get a description of the long-term impact of his Deer Hill experience. He wrote back that same day:

It's hard to remember the exact way the world seemed to me after my junior year of high school, but I do know I had a big mouth (still do). It wasn't so much that I would be honest, as much as it was my propensity to say something that I knew would get me noticed. If someone made a mistake and I knew the answer, I'd make a joke to show that I did in such a way that emphasized that they didn't. Loudly. I guess I liked to needle people.

That's when my folks, at a loss as of what to do to get me on the right path (the one where you think of other people, listen and become something other than a drain on the human race as a whole), took me to see "you know who." I knew little of you at the time, except for your stern eyes and an air about you that said, "Don't mess with me." I remember after meeting all of us, you asked my parents to leave so you and I could have a more frank discussion. We did, at which point you promised me that nothing about my summer would be decided that day. You probably now deny that happened.

Ha! Actually he's right, I thought to myself, as I continued reading.

Then you met with my parents. When we all sat down together, I knew that that agreement would not be honored. I was angry and held on to the fact that I had been "lied to" by you.

That resentment and clinging on to small things followed me to dorky Colorado. If the phone didn't work, if there wasn't any dessert, if the mail didn't come in, or any other small item, I started a campaign. How could I be expected to participate in this program I didn't want in the first place without getting what I had been told I would receive?

I looked up from the computer and looked out the window and smiled to myself. How maddening and yet how wonderful teenagers can be!

I took aim at the biggest target I could find. It just so happened that he was the director of the program and quite literally the biggest person there. 6'5" with a slow, calm disposition and kind eyes that looked right through you.

I can remember him averting his gaze as I spouted off on my latest diatribe about having to do the dishes. Though I only saw Doug for a total of four or five days when we were transitioning from the field back to base camp, I oscillated between being friendly with him and taking direct aim at his program.

This sounded strange, I had known Doug for 20 years and couldn't imagine him averting his eyes from anyone. As I read on, I felt a rush of emotion.

> I enjoyed most of the time in the field. The people we worked with and the diversity of the program gave me a new perspective to life. I certainly knew that not everyone was as lucky as I, but to hear the details and get to know some very nice folks, I think they were Summer Search kids who had different kind of expectations for what the world would give them, which was refreshing. Everyone had their struggles, but some of the scholarship students had problems that never occurred to me. I remember the guilt that I felt for my privilege many times there, and perhaps this was the beginning of coming to terms with the world in which I was raised.

We were getting there, the beginning of compassion. Yet Benji couldn't stop his adolescent self from jabbing.

> On the last few days, I again took aim at Doug about not letting us kids call home. To this day, I'm not sure if he targeted just me by disallowing phone use, but he succeeded in reeling me in. I was loud and encouraged others to speak to him privately to support my cause. In the midst of my mobilization, Doug strolled up from the cafeteria. I yelled to him something about the absurdity of the situation. He didn't acknowledge the words. He kept walking.

Doug must have been at his wit's end—and I would have been, too. It was time to expand my enquiry. Without sending him Benji's description, I emailed Doug and asked him to write back specifically what had happened as best as he could remember. Like Benji, he responded immediately:

> What do you do with a 17-year-old participant who is older, smarter, and more capable than his peers in the group? And who is also a wise guy as well as negative leader? For

three weeks, I had heard about this young man who didn't want to be at Deer Hill. He was sent against his will by his parents and he was going to make sure everyone knew it. He was clever, funny, and well-liked by the others because he was cool.

I'll tell you exactly what I did. Toward the end of the trip while I was in the cafeteria, he started in again about the lack of phone access. I'd finally had enough. I turned around and said, "Can we talk privately?" He responded with one of his smartass remarks, saying, "Is this going to be some sort of kumbaya moment?"

We ended up in the old woodshop before I let him have it. "I have scratched and clawed to be able to create this place, a place that you, someone with very little life experience, have thought fit to knock down. You haven't taken one minute to look around you and realize that this place you have been ripping down to everyone is my dream." He started to cry but stuffed it and tossed off some other smart remark. That's when I lost it and roared, "How dare you belittle what I have labored on for so long to create? Who are you to mock my dream of guiding young people to discover their own courage and their own voice?" That's when I grabbed him, and we both began to cry.

It was fascinating that almost 10 years later this incident was so vivid, so fresh in both of their minds. And that, in retelling this story, their memories so exactly dovetailed. Benji ended his email to me with:

After I yelled out to him in the cafeteria, that's when Doug started rapping on me. He said that since I had gotten there I hadn't taken one second to realize that this place that I had been ripping down to everyone was his dream. I tried to say something sarcastic but I couldn't get a single word out. Then Doug grabbed and held me. It's hard to say how long we stood there in that shed but the effect still lasts today. I left Doug with a soaking shirt and so very sorry for my lack of awareness.

Benji concluded his email with a question.

How applicable was that moment to the rest of my life?

Benji's father, Don, told me that Benji wrote about Doug—the person he most admired—in his college applications.

For Doug, that confrontation in the woodshed reinforced the deeply felt values that fueled his dream. For Benji the answer to his question was:

> I'd say the effects are far-ranging. Though I still am loud and outspoken, I try to look around and put myself in others' shoes. I don't always, but I certainly feel better about who I have become.

For both Benji and Doug, this chance to remember, reflect back, and recount their story, became another opportunity to think new thoughts. How did it end?

A few weeks later, the phone rang. A voice thick with emotion was saying, "Benji called me today." Doug choked up for a few seconds before continuing. "He has decided to create an annual scholarship so a low-income student can learn what he learned at Deer Hill, and he is sending a check for $1,000! *He wants other kids to have the chance to speak from the heart and listen with respect.*"

| four |

The Interview

In the history of the world, no one ever washed a rental car.

—Larry Summers

By 1995, the fifth year of operation, Summer Search was finally stable and credible. The funding was steady, the referral sources were dedicated and highly committed, and the students were starting to become role models and little beacons of light in their schools and communities. And I was learning how to structure the important initial interview.

In spite of my years in private practice, translating standard interviewing methods into a new format had proved challenging. Finding the balance between moving quickly through an interview to get enough information while giving space to talk and be heard took time. As the program became more well-known and the number of students multiplied, it became harder to reject students. At the same time, it was also critical that I select students who could benefit from the experiences and challenges that Summer Search had to offer. Most kids had an unrealistic view of what Summer Search actually

45

was as they tended to focus on the "free trip" part. What too often got left out was "going for hard."

I decided to expand the purpose of the interview beyond admission or rejection into Summer Search. What about the interview could become valuable for every student? Maybe to learn something new about themselves? This wasn't as hard as I initially imagined. I merely had to ask the students themselves to answer that question, and although many of their answers were predictable they were also often surprising.

Yet the workload was crushing. In spite of the rush I experienced with each new youngster, it was getting harder to approach interviewing season with the same vigor. Two calls within a week of each other changed everything.

It was late afternoon at the office, and I was just getting ready to head home when the phone rang. It was Jay Jacobs, the nephew of Carol Tolan, a committed Summer Search donor. "I'm graduating with a degree in divinity from Harvard and I've been thinking a lot about what I want to do…" He laughed. "Obviously." There was an uncomfortable pause. "So I've decided not to pursue the ministry." Then with more energy he said, "I'm fascinated by your program. In fact, I'm wondering about starting Summer Search here in Boston."

Jay Jacobs had been a leader with one of my favorite programs, NOLS, and there had been two Summer Search kids in one of the groups he had led on a particularly difficult expedition in Alaska. He was blown away by the concept and the reality of offering students from underprivileged backgrounds a shot at the kinds of opportunities usually available only to the highly privileged.

My first impulse was to put Jay off, which I did. It was just too much to think about. Later that week, the phone rang again. This time, it was a young woman from Pittsburgh named Katherine Calihan. My husband gave a speech to an organization her parents had joined and afterwards we went to their home for dinner. At that time Katherine was sick in bed with the flu so we met only briefly —but I liked her immediately. She was young and unformed, but I sensed an internal strength. An old-fashioned word came to mind: plucky.

As I grew to know Katherine better, my hunch about this "plucky" girl was borne out. She called me her sophomore year of college asking about a summer program that would get her out of her comfortable surroundings, both at home and at school. She ended up spending three months that summer in a community service program in Kenya, living with a family in a home without electricity while teaching in the local school. When she returned to college, she changed her major to African American studies.

After graduating from college, she called to tell me she had just been accepted to an innovative, relatively new program called Teach for America. Candidates had to be willing to teach in understaffed inner-city or rural schools. She wondered about working for Summer Search, but as we talked more, Katherine realized that she needed to take on this challenge. She spent the next two years teaching at a middle school in inner-city Baltimore.

The call today was different. After some small talk, Katherine said, "I know you won't believe this, but ever since high school I've wanted to work with you." She was right: I was surprised. Yet there had been that immediate chemistry between us; I felt an inner twinge. "I have a part-time secretary but I've always worked mostly alone," I told her. "Plus, I'm not sure about teaching someone else, especially about interviewing and mentoring."

Katherine was not so easily brushed off. "Can I fly out for a few days and just talk with you?" I paused for a moment. Why not? And then, since I was already opening that door, I decided to call Jay in Boston and invite him for a visit the following week.

When I picked up Katherine at the airport, she was older and seemed much more mature. With her blonde hair, athletic body, and green eyes, she had become a striking-looking young woman. On the trip home, she began talking passionately about how hard the last two years had been. Fighting the educational bureaucracy in Baltimore while simultaneously trying to inspire energetic sixth and seventh graders, most of whom faced challenging health issues and learning difficulties, had been an uphill battle. As I listened, it was clear that she had acquired a new depth and confidence that only added to her inherent pluck.

At seven the next morning, we headed off to Lowell High School. Founded in 1856, Lowell was the first public high school west of the Mississippi. Today, it is the only public school in San Francisco where entrance is merit-based and highly competitive. The school's population is 58 percent Asian American, and 40 percent of the students are low-income.[1]

On the long drive over, I made calls to summer program directors on the East Coast, trying to wrangle scholarships for the new students I'd just accepted. Katherine got to see some Indiana-style horse-trading in action. In spite of myself, I wanted to impress her, so I tried to stifle the Midwestern accent that tended to creep in at these moments. It was an odd, yet good feeling to have company on what would otherwise have been a tedious and lonely drive.

Lowell's long hallways were quiet and clean, perhaps only because the majority of students had yet to arrive. An exhausted-looking referring counselor with heavy bags under her eyes was waiting for us. She had lots of candidates, most of them Asian, but she had also made a real effort to target and refer under-represented students at Lowell, which meant African American and Latino. "I do have one

---

1. San Francisco Unified School District School Accountability Report Card. School year 2012–2013.

African American boy. He has a bit of an attitude, his grades are mostly Cs, but he excels in French." My eyes widened in surprise, and she smiled. "Interesting, huh? I think you're going to like him. His name is..." she paused, "Roy Rogers."

Katherine and I settled into a dusty extra room that was, as usual, lined with stacks of unused computer equipment. I spread out the tools of the trade: first and most importantly, the box of tissues. "When you ask simple, open-ended questions and then just listen, the interviews often get emotional fairly quickly," I told her. She looked at me and started to ask something as I continued, "The chairs need to be placed at an angle, so if it gets too intense kids can break eye contact and look away." I smiled, "Sounds like therapy, huh?"

I realized that I needed to explain the process more carefully and said, "Although I use a few of the same therapeutic techniques from my private practice, it's important to emphasize that these interviews are not therapy: just a chance for kids to let us see things from their perspective, their chance to let us 'walk in their shoes.'" Katherine's expressive eyes, which could flicker from green to yellow, lit up. I could feel her excitement.

I smiled and continued: "To simplify a very complicated process, I usually ask just three questions: tell me about your summers, tell me about school, and tell me about your family. Oh, I recently decided to expand the interview beyond getting or not getting a scholarship. I now tell every student that another important goal is to learn something new about themselves. This focuses them on telling their story. Anyway, asking about summer gets the interview going on a somewhat neutral topic, and it can provide useful information about each student's level of opportunity. For example, did they go to Japan on some special program last summer, or did they stay home to take care of a disabled sibling, or did they work all summer and give most of their income to help their family?"

Katherine nodded as I continued. "Asking about school gives you information about performance. How motivated and how effective is this student? The most important information has to do with school attendance and grades. Statistics show pretty conclusively that students who are absent during the early part of high school are much less likely to graduate.[2] Grades are trickier. There is no GPA requirement to be accepted to Summer Search, but if a student's grades are low, we need to know why. Is it a lack of discipline or internal interference? Or is it because they have adult responsibilities at home—like being a wage earner or being the translator for their family?"

I looked at Katherine and smiled again. She was so energetic and interested. This was fun. I continued: "Always take careful note of the student's first response about school. From the past five years of experience, I've learned that if it's negative—'school sucks' or 'the teachers here are unfair'—it's a strong indicator that the student is not a candidate. Also, students who don't think they are successful *anywhere* or good at *anything* are usually not candidates. If you hear one or both of those things, then it's important to shift gears and make the interview less emotional. You don't want kids to open up and become too vulnerable, only to be rejected."

"How can you find that out so quickly?"

"Always write down the first thing a student says when you ask him or her about school." There was a knock on the door, so I finished in a whisper. "The final question, 'Tell me about your family,' is where the interview gets emotional. But I think we should stop for now."

---

2. Elaine M. Allensworth and John Q. Easton. What matters for staying on track and graduating in Chicago Public High School: a close look at course grades, failures, attendance in the freshman year. Chicago: Consortium on Chicago School Research. 2007.

Katherine started to ask another question, but she was cut off as a small Asian girl walked in. In the early '90s there was a flood of immigrants from Southeast Asia to the Bay Area. Most were extremely low-income and supported by AFDC (Aid for Families of Dependent Children). This girl looked poor. Her skin was pale and spotted with blemishes; her clothes looked worn and her short hair greasy. She sat down in the empty chair at the head of the table and, before even mentioning her name, told us her GPA was 3.7. Then she began telling us what it was like to walk in her shoes. So much for the three questions! Within 10 minutes, she was crying and sharing her deepest anxieties. Her parents emigrated from Vietnam and didn't speak English, their apartment had been broken into four times, and she lived in a chronic state of emotional and physical terror for herself and her family. Her name was Chai.

As Chai bravely took advantage of this unique moment to share her pain and traumas with a stranger whose scholarship program she already guessed had the potential to change her life, I started thinking about where to place her that summer. An idea popped in: Longacre Farm. The director, Susan Smith, had called recently to say there was room for three more students. Although she wanted boys since I had found two boys, I was sure she would take this girl. The emphasis at the farm was on building community through participation in daily group sessions which would be perfect for Chai.

Chai paused to catch her breath and looked at us expectantly. Then her eyes widened and her face tightened. What was going to happen next? I looked her in the eye and told her she had done a very good job of putting us in her shoes. "So, Chai, what did you learn about yourself in this interview?"

"I learned I can tell my story to strangers," she said without hesitation.

Indeed she did. I turned to Katherine and said, "The Longacre program promotes leadership qualities through teaching teenagers to communicate with each other in meaningful ways through daily group meetings. This young woman could clearly use such an outlet."

I handed Chai a brochure, along with our new student handbook with step-by-step directions for joining the program. She looked at me blankly. "You are now a Summer Search student," I said, squeezing her hand. Chai opened the brightly colored brochure slowly. As she read a quick description of the trip, she blurted out, "I don't know anything about farming."

"How are we going to solve that problem?"

Chai looked puzzled, and then said, "Well, I guess I'll just have to learn!" As she got up to go, she beamed at Katherine. "Thank you."

After Chai left, Katherine asked, "Do you always make decisions so quickly?" Before I could answer, she added, "And these interviews—are they always so emotional?"

"Remember, Katherine, students are nominated by a referral source who understands the program and usually knows what we look for. After that, if the nominated students want an interview, all they have to do is write a one-page essay. Most do not."

Katherine interrupted, "Really? Why? I don't understand."

"I have trouble understanding that one too," I said. I glanced at my watch—there was so much to explain—before continuing: "A psychologist from Berkeley, now deceased, Lillian Ruben, wrote about 'triumphant children'—meaning young people who have been able to somehow overcome significant trauma.[3] Today we would describe them as resilient children or those who have 'grit.' Anyway, one of their most striking qualities is their ability to separate themselves from their parents. You can actually see that in speaking to groups

3.   Rubin, Lillian B. *The Transcendent Child: Tales of Triumph Over the Pond.* New York NY Basic Books. 1996.

of kids about Summer Search. When you talk about separating from home there are those whose eyes light up and those who immediately check out as they decide the program is not for them."

"How about in the actual interview?" Katherine asked.

"Kids like Chai who make a sudden and courageous decision to share their lives are able to risk becoming emotionally vulnerable. This demonstrates a kind of strength. In psychiatry, we call it 'ego strength.'"

"I understand the word *ego*, but what exactly do you mean by it here?" asked Katherine.

"It's hard to describe," I answered, aware of how vague I sounded. I paused to focus my thoughts. "The kids who are able to make such a sudden investment, to see the interview as a chance to put their thoughts and feelings on the table—sometimes for the first time ever—are able to make a certain leap of faith."

Our conversation ended abruptly as the next student arrived. As soon as he stepped through the door, I knew who it was: Roy Rogers. He was big, slightly overweight, and right away I recognized that attitude the teacher had told us about. As he sat down, he gave both of us an appraising look, then followed it up with a disarming smile. "How are you ladies doing today?" Yes, he was cocky. Still, there was something—a certain charisma and charm. I liked him, and looking at Katherine it seemed that she did too.

This time, I got to tell him about the additional goal of the interview as well as ask the three questions. Last summer, Roy had worked at a fast-food place and used the money for school expenses. His performance in school was interesting. Though he was obviously smart, he had just a C average overall. But, just as his counselor had said, he got an A in French. I was intrigued by the gap between his ability and his performance, so I decided to push him. "You're clearly smart, Roy; so why do you think you get such mediocre grades?"

"I don't know, I get bored or something."

"Are you interested in finding out why?"

"Sure." He stared at me and I stared back. There was a silence. Then he said, "Yeah, I guess I am."

"Guess? Are you or aren't you?"

Roy looked at me again for a long second, his eyes strangely blank.

"Tell us about your family," I continued.

"My parents both work and…my dad, he doesn't live with us anymore." There was a short pause. "My sister, she goes to UCLA right now."

The energy level of the interview suddenly dropped.

I wondered what to do. "Roy, we don't want to pry. Unless you really want to describe what your family life is like, I don't think I will ask any more specific questions. Well, maybe there is one—I guess I am wondering why it is so challenging for you to talk frankly about yourself and your family."

He was silent. "We just don't talk that much at home. I'm not used to this."

"Tell you what, Roy, I can tell it's been hard but that's the whole point of this interview—the opportunity to speak openly and honestly. In spite of the fact that you didn't take much of a risk here," I added, "we're still going to take a risk on you."

Roy's head snapped up, and his eyes momentarily lost that blank look as I continued. "There's a wonderful trip to France with a program called Choate Rosemary Hall. Students study French while living with a family for five weeks. It's expensive, almost $5,000. Choate will give Summer Search a scholarship, but in return I have to guarantee an outstanding student, meaning someone who doesn't have an attitude. Do you think that's you?"

"Yeah." Then he surprised me and said, "Actually, I don't know."

"That's honest. I admire that. Think it over, and if you are that person, call me within five days, and we will do another interview."

As he started to get up, I said, "Almost forgot. What is new that you learned about yourself today?"

"I learned that I have trouble talking about myself."

"You know that already. What did you learn that was new?"

Roy's eyes cast about—anywhere but into mine. "I learned that I'm afraid but I don't know why."

"Roy, that was honest and brave and maybe you will figure that out. Thank you."

After Roy left, Katherine was bursting with questions. "He didn't seem to open up at all, let alone get emotional. Why did you offer him such a major scholarship?"

"Even though he is underperforming in school, my hunch is that he has tremendous potential. It is very rare for a student to excel in a foreign language. He also had an unusual honesty—like when he admitted he wasn't sure about his attitude. And how about what he learned? Yes, for some reason, he's afraid of looking too closely at himself. When students mention an older sibling, always ask about that sibling's level of performance. A sister at UCLA is pretty intimidating. Maybe he pulls back because he is afraid he won't measure up to her, or maybe being under the gun constantly at this school—Lowell is so competitive—has made him defensive. I don't know. But let's give him a chance and see what happens."

"What do you think will happen next?" Katherine asked.

Glad to be able to answer more specifically, I said, "There is a post-interview process that allows me to take risks. If students are not highly motivated, that process causes them to drop out. I'm betting that the odds on Roy calling are 50/50. Actually I'm more pessimistic—I'd say it's 60/40 that he won't call at all. Remember, we're sending kids off to take huge risks in alien places. We are asking them to join groups of affluent students. They will initially feel like outsiders because of race and economic deprivation, or they might also be literally outsiders because they're immigrants. It's a scary proposition."

"But how you can predict who will and who won't follow through?"

"Good question. Some kids are initially afraid of the physical demands, but when they learn more about it, they become even more afraid of the emotional demands. And then there are those kids who are afraid of succeeding."

Katherine jumped. "I saw this all the time with the kids I taught in Baltimore! They would work so hard and then as soon as they achieved something, succeeded at something, they would lose energy and blow it. I never knew why or what to do." She paused, and looked at me with real urgency. "How can we help them?"

"It's important to remember that the behavior we are talking about is unconscious. Our goal, just like any good therapist's, is to make the unconscious conscious. None of us can change behaviors we can't see."

Katherine leaned forward. "But I'm not a therapist."

It was challenging to explain what I had never put into words before, but it was also stimulating to think out loud in this way. "You are not a therapist," I said, "and Summer Search is not therapy. But that doesn't mean that we can't learn to use certain tools and basics, like how to help kids tell their story, retell it, and start to see that repetitious, self-defeating behaviors don't make sense. Once they see that, then slowly over time we can help them begin to understand where those behaviors came from, and they can begin to rewrite their story."

Katherine nodded slowly as I continued. "For your middle-school students, that's not possible. Studies show that the brains of kids that age are not yet developed for the abstract thinking and the complicated work of introspection. With adolescents, it's different."

By early afternoon, Katherine was getting restless. I could tell that interviewing seemed relatively easy to her, so I asked her if she wanted to try. She instantly agreed. Before she started, I clarified that we had to be straight with the students, and explain who she was and why she was with me. We also needed to ask their permission.

The next student, another Asian girl, walked into the room, and Katherine introduced herself with poise and confidence. They got through the shoes part and the summer part, but then something happened. In talking about school, the student's first answer was she didn't like her school; the teachers and the other students were mean. Katherine wrote this down. Then the rest of her answers gradually lapsed into yeses and nos.

"How are you feeling about your interview?" I interrupted.

"I don't want to talk about my family," she answered.

"That's okay. You should be proud of being nominated. We ask our teachers to look for a special spark. What do you think they saw in you?"

The student wasn't sure. Then I asked her what she had learned about herself from the interview. She wasn't sure about that either but promised to think about it.

Katherine was flushed. "What just happened?"

"It's important to recognize when a student doesn't want to go forward with the interview—and they will let you know. Manage in the moment, respond to what you see. As for the rest, good interviewing looks simple but is difficult to execute. I've been at this for five years now and before that, for 20 years in a counseling practice. The main thing is to keep your questions open-ended, like, 'Tell me about school?'"

"I did ask her about school."

"No, you asked her about grades. She said *A*s and *B*s. Then you asked about her best subject, and she said 'history.' Do you see the difference? The other thing to remember is to think in terms of opposites. When a student is vague ask for specifics, but when they go on and on with details ask them to summarize."

Katherine looked thoughtful as I concluded. "If the student makes the decision to drive the interview, that frees you up to be the listener. If they don't make that decision, that is their choice."

The door opened unexpectedly. A tall, athletic-looking African American boy entered the room and told us his name was Tyrone. He was referred at the last minute and handed me an essay he had just written. He then moved fairly easily through the elements of the interview and ended up talking fairly specifically about his family history. Despite significant challenges at home (his father left early on and his mother was an alcoholic), he was a good student and talented baseball player.

After a shorter interview than usual, I told him that I thought he was a candidate for the program and handed him a brochure for an extended wilderness expedition, always the ideal first step.

Tyrone hesitated. "Actually, what I want to do is travel out of the country or maybe go to Hawaii."

"Oh? Really? I'm not big on trips to Hawaii."

"That's okay, I promised my coach I would work for him the whole summer, anyway. Maybe I'll take one of your scholarships next year."

"Wait. You mean you already had another commitment?" I looked at him incredulously. There was a long silence before I added, "In other words, you misrepresented yourself. You might even say that you didn't tell us the truth."

"I just thought I'd see what I could get."

"This program is not just about 'getting' scholarships, it's about being truthful and honoring your commitments." There was another long, uncomfortable pause. He shifted in his chair and looked down.

I realized to be fair I needed to give him a chance to respond. "What are you learning about yourself so far?" He didn't answer. "Do you want to say anything?"

He jumped up, shot me a disgusted look, and with his back turned, mumbled, "Screw you, lady," then left, slamming the door behind him.

I sucked in my breath.

"You don't much care about what other people think of you, do you?" Katherine asked. I blinked my eyes and tried to clear my thoughts. "Don't you think you were a little harsh? You even called him a liar."

I was not used to this kind of questioning and replied as evenly as I could. "Sometimes I am." But wait, I did not call him a liar. Never use words that could be perceived as name calling, like selfish or liar. Stick to the facts. He didn't tell the full truth.

Katherine didn't respond. Already she was learning to wait, so that I was suddenly in the unusual position of needing to explain myself. "Your question, and the kind of self-examination it asks for is good." I realized this sounded defensive, so I switched gears. "In this case, we only had one shot to impress that young man. Either he'll blow it off, or he will learn something and never again treat his commitments so casually. Who knows? Maybe he'll have the courage to show up next year. If he does, I'll interview him again."

Katherine looked thoughtful, but there was no time for more questions: we had to pack up and give the referring counselor a report on the day. As we walked down the now empty hallway, I told her, "When you confront a kid like that, always leave room for them to come back with a rebuttal. I did, but his choice was unfortunate."

As soon as we were back in the car, Katherine smiled, "I just have one question right now." She paused, "How many kids are successful in Summer Search?"

"Remember this is year five," I paused to think before continuing. "The first two years I wasn't sure about how to select, how to follow up. So almost all the kids finished their trips but quite a few dropped out after that, maybe 50 percent. That is changing largely because of many of the things I'm telling you today." Katherine smiled, then as was her habit, said directly, "I want to work with you."

I weighed the pros and cons for less than a minute. Yes, it would be hard to run the program and mentor a young adult at the same time. But, if Summer Search was going to grow and live beyond me, this step was essential. Katherine was intuitive and bright, and, yes, stubborn and cheeky. I decided to make the same leap of faith I asked of the kids. "Katherine," I said, "Welcome aboard. You and I are going to have a lot to learn."

* * *

The following week, Jay Jacobs arrived. It was exciting to meet this unassuming young man who had brown hair that refused to behave and a face that radiated kindness and sincerity. From the first moment, however, it was clear that either he didn't possess Katherine's confidence, or he was able to see the magnitude of the task more clearly. There was a certain reserve. He spent the night at our office in Mill Valley, which had a small bedroom and kitchen. When I picked him up at 6:30 the next morning, he seemed fresh and eager to tackle a day of interviewing. His main questions were about the interview. All the post-trip student essays seemed to focus on that explosive moment. "What exactly happens in that interview?" Jay asked. He certainly had done his homework.

At Oakland Tech, we inched the car through the maze of sullen-looking kids walking slowly while blocking the entry to the gated parking lot. Once inside there was an empty police car with the doors flung open wide. "The officers must have been in a hurry," I observed. Jay's face remained the same but he shifted in his seat, reminding me of how scared I was going to these schools in the beginning.

We made our way cautiously through the tumultuous hallways to a large and suddenly quiet room. A team of two veteran teachers, a man and woman, one senior, and three new students sat waiting. As we prepared to begin our interviews in a small, unventilated room made even smaller by a clutter of miscellaneous materials, I explained to Jay the standard setup: tissues, water, and seating. He looked interested but didn't ask any questions, which only made me more curious to know what he was thinking.

Che, the one senior who had already successfully participated in two trips, came in first. Before he sat down, he started telling me that he was hopeful that his mother's lengthy jail sentence for manufacturing amphetamines would be shortened. I interrupted and asked him if he would feel comfortable summarizing his history for Jay.

He turned to Jay and began to retell his story. I was pleased and proud that basic trust could be transferred so effortlessly. After Che left, Jay looked at me. The excitement in his eyes was visible. For the first time, I felt like I knew what he was feeling. "I can't believe how comfortable that young man was talking about such difficult things!" Jay exclaimed. "I mean, how does this happen?"

"Let's get a few interviews under our belt, and then we'll talk," I replied.

The morning, however, was discouraging. The next three students understandably wanted to escape their difficult lives, but they didn't have any special interests or a track record of sticking with anything. Their grades were poor to average and school attendance spotty, always a real worry. At least this gave me the opportunity to explain to Jay how destructive it was to send kids into situations and trips they didn't have the strength to handle. Being slammed by another failure was the last thing these young people needed. Just as we were packing up to leave, I heard the door rattle; a skinny African American boy walked in with his head down. It was Monroe! How could I have forgotten him?

In our first interview, the year before, Monroe had sat silently, unable to look me in the eye. In his messy initial essay, he wrote, "Before the bad things happened, I knew I was really, really smart." I kept asking him to look at me, but he wouldn't or maybe couldn't. Finally, I sat down on the floor in the exact spot he focused on so intently. He was accepted into the program and did well on a very challenging Outward Bound program. Then he came home and disappeared.

"So, Monroe," I said, scrutinizing him closely now. "This is Jay Jacobs. He's thinking of starting a Summer Search program in Boston." Monroe didn't look at Jay and mumbled something while handing me a dirty, crumpled piece of paper.

"What's this?"

"My final essay."

"This isn't even close, and you know it," I said, glancing at the paper and then handing it to Jay.

"Let's talk about the year, Monroe. As best as I can recollect, it seems that you've done everything wrong."

Monroe stared at me for a few long seconds before looking down and replying, "Yes, ma'am, I guess I did."

"Let's see if we can be sure. First, you didn't call in when you returned from Outward Bound, right? In fact, I had to call you. Then you didn't write your Summer Search post-trip essay, which was due over six months ago. Oh, and you didn't show up for the Fall Event to celebrate your success. Let me tell you, Monroe, that one really broke my heart. Worst of all, you didn't bother to return my telephone calls. Who do you think you are?"

I paused to let this sink in while the silence built. "Oh, yes, and now, to top it off, you show up now with this half-hearted, dare I say, half-assed essay? Did I get it straight?"

There was a short silence interrupted by a soft, "Yeah."

"That's a lot of things to screw up, don't you think?" Out of the corner of my eye, I caught a glimpse of Jay's concerned face. "I mean, given how smart you are, you had to be paying close attention or you might have done something right...*accidentally*. You know?"

The corner of Monroe's mouth twitched slightly. I frowned and pushed on. "Not following through on every single commitment takes concentration." There was another long pause. "Don't you agree?"

Monroe looked down but didn't respond. I turned to Jay and said, "What do you think we should do?" Jay, who was by now starting to smile, just shrugged.

"Well, then I'll ask you again, Monroe. What should I do?"

"I think you should kick me out of the program."

"Ha!" I glanced at Jay. "Well, I won't do it. This isn't my program, Monroe, it's your program. You'll have to kick yourself out. So far you are doing an excellent job at doing just that. But I warn you, if you stay, you also have to take responsibility for yourself. For starters, throw this paper away and write a decent essay."

Monroe was giving darting looks at me from the corner of his eyes. After a long silence, he finally said, "I don't know what to do."

"Sorry, pal, me neither. You did do a good job on your Outward Bound course, which was really hard. I was so proud of you. Now I have another trip in mind. You take Spanish, right? I'm thinking of something like a community service trip in a Spanish-speaking country, say, like Costa Rica. But I can't make that choice for you. Going forward or falling back, that's your call, not mine."

Monroe sat for another long moment immobilized. Finally, I said, "Think about it. Send in a decent essay and call me in one week if you want to be back on board." As I hugged his stiff body, I said, "Remember one other thing. If you ever again don't return my telephone calls, you are one dead man."

Monroe stood up, and as he walked out the door, he broke into an involuntary grin.

Before I could get myself together, Jay exclaimed, "This program is pretty damned exciting! But when should I give a student another chance?"

"Oh, I don't know," I said, distracted. I looked at Jay's eager face. "These questions are good but also very complicated. Monroe's grades were terrible, but believe it or not, he is sitting on tremendous brainpower. He's also very kind."

Jay leaned forward as I continued. "Monroe has also been a victim of horrible neglect. His mother was a drug addict and couldn't take care of him and his younger siblings. Currently, they are living with his grandmother."

Jay's expression told me he wasn't connecting to what I was saying. I paused to put my thoughts together. "There are two reasons I took him on. First, he is altruistic: when things began to fall apart, he was the one in the family who tried to take care of the others. And although he is failing math, his PSAT scores are the highest in the sophomore class."

"But why did you treat him like that?"

"Oh. Well. Okay, here it is. After students have a huge success when they finish their first summer program, coming home they will often pull back. They just aren't used to feeling so positive about themselves." The pathos of Monroe's history hit me. To my surprise, I found myself tearing up. "Push, criticize, and confront—but always support."

Jay's face had the blank look that showed he still wasn't connecting to what I was saying. I cast about. "Never hit a kid who has been hit."

His eyes widened. "What I mean is that students who are manipulative need to be confronted directly but kids who have been abused like Monroe need to be confronted, but in a different way. They will constantly push for rejection. Yes, you have to respond to and confront their self-defeating behaviors, but at the same time avoid the trap of rejecting them. Don't let them seduce you into making that decision. Make them take the responsibility for their mistakes. Now, that said, I have gone the distance with Monroe—he will either step up to the plate or disappear—but again, it's essential that this be his choice, not mine."

Jay's expressive face turned thoughtful.

Monroe did decide to follow through and rewrote his essay, barely. He began to call in more frequently and went to Costa Rica the following summer. After his trip at the Fall Event at Oakland High, he not only showed up but won an award for his final essay. Today he has a family and a successful career in the Navy.

* * *

The next morning as we headed off to another troubled high school in southeast San Francisco, Jay had begun to relax. He was ready to try his hand at interviewing and had carefully prepared the exact interview format I used the day before.

Although his intelligence and quick grasp of complicated material were impressive, the interviews didn't progress. Each student was different, but Jay stuck to the script rather than reacting to the student in front of him. Within a few minutes, the kids lapsed into single word answers. As I watched his face, I saw sweat break out on his brow. This lack of progress was clearly distressing to him.

The rest of the day passed slowly. The students seemed to instinctively trust him, but they were puzzled by his lack of clarity and direction.

As I listened, I realized something. I trusted him, too. It was time to take another leap of faith. "Jay, if you are interested in working closely in an ongoing mentoring relationship with me, I think you are the right person to start our first satellite office in Boston."

He looked surprised. I continued with a smile, "Your instincts are good, you care more about the students than yourself. And guess what? Just last week I received another anonymous grant from a prestigious foundation for $25,000. They have been supporting me for four years, but their goal is funding good programs and then helping them expand. If I don't replicate Summer Search in another city or area, they will move on."

Before Jay could respond, the final student, an energetic Mexican American sophomore wearing heavy eye makeup, almost bounced into the room smiling. She was ready to talk and told Jay very specifically what it was like to walk in her precarious platform shoes. His questions were simpler and clearer. Gradually, she felt safe enough to shed a few tears as she described her difficult family life. She learned that she could feel safe in telling her story.

And so, we became a team, but it wasn't easy. For Jay and Katherine to confront their students' negative messages about themselves, they had to tackle their own. Katherine was a smoker; I too smoked at her age, but she quit (no small feat). Then she began to think about why she started in the first place. She was raised in a Catholic household, surrounded by *shoulds* and *shouldn'ts*. Given a new way of looking at behaviors, Katherine began to understand that smoking was one of the ways she rebelled and that her rebelliousness was a necessary part of her journey toward finding her own voice.

We soon identified the origins of Jay's emotional remoteness. He was the product of a stoic New England Presbyterian household. But why was he so careful? Together, we gradually explored the source of his performance anxiety. When Jay was in his preteens, something happened in his family. His father, a Princeton graduate, dropped out of a promising career in his early 30s and became the bus driver for the local school. This was not only embarrassing, but deep down Jay was haunted by the fear that something unknown would happen in his own career. Something unexpected would derail him too. Once this connection was made, Jay began to breathe easier.

As for me, I learned that I could teach the complicated interview process. It could be transferred! This decision was going to ensure that more students would have the unique opportunity of telling and retelling their stories and rewriting the narratives of their lives into something larger, more flexible, and ultimately more satisfying.

For Katherine and Jay, the Summer Search method of dishing out direct feedback was something they not only survived but began to embrace. Soon they started experiencing the unique freedom that accompanies an examined life. Gradually, the three of us developed an intimate relationship based on a foundation of mutual understanding, deep trust, and, yes, mutual vulnerability.

There was a shadow. I had no idea how vulnerable I was going to become, as Summer Search developed into something larger, much larger than us all.

| five |

Insight Mentoring

The sound of the genuine in yourself is the only true guide you will ever have. If you cannot hear it, you will, all of your life, spend your days on the end of strings that somebody else pulls.

—Howard Thurman

One of the great mysteries of human behavior is why some people change, but others do not. What allows one person to tell, retell, and rewrite his or her story? And why do so many others live out the same unchanging, limited script over and over?

After 20 years in a private counseling practice and another 20 years of directing Summer Search, I found three major factors that impact change: the mentors we choose, the degree of pain we feel, and our ability to look inward as the conduit for change/transformation.

Jerome Kagan, a retired psychologist from Harvard, writes that there are six major developmental factors that profoundly influence our lives: genetic material, early childhood experiences, birth order, generation in which we come of age, luck, and mentors.[1]

---

1. Kagan, Jerome. *The Temperamental Thread: How Genes, Culture, Time, and Luck Made Us Who We Are.* New York: Dana Press. 2010.

There's something interesting about this list. Our genetic makeup, what happens in early childhood (governed by one's parents), birth order, and the generation in which we come of age are all predetermined. And luck is random and also out of our control. There is just one major developmental factor over which we have any control: *mentors*.

The mentors we choose can reinforce our programmed ideas about ourselves, or they can become powerful forces for healing and change. I had two who stand out. The first was an English teacher at my public high school in Muncie, Indiana. Growing up on a farm, I knew few people with a passion for reading. My father's only interest was *Thoroughbred Record* magazine, a monthly account of horse racing in the U.S.; my mother used reading to escape. A dedicated English teacher, Mr. Langdon, exposed me to the world of English literature. Sensing my interest and gratitude, he gave me a list of great books to read, most of which I did. His love for literature soon became mine.

Another important mentor was an older nurse named Alma. I was fresh out of training and counted myself lucky to land a position at the Langley Porter Psychiatric Institute, a teaching and training hospital at the University of California Medical Center in San Francisco. Alma, a sarcastic, brilliant, chain-smoking lesbian was my supervisor. I can still see her sitting in the nursing station carefully preparing her cigarettes in that special holder she had and then slowly blowing smoke in the air as she talked. She taught me how to work calmly in challenging situations with very sick individuals— patients who might suddenly lash out and even strike me, patients who were manic and severely agitated, or, more rarely, patients who were catatonic and immobilized.

Alma's greatest gift was helping me understand why self-destructive behaviors so often repeat. Most of our patients were unconsciously programmed to see themselves as victims. Somewhat unsympathetically, Alma described them as people who "love to suffer." Victims, she would say, "can't heal themselves because they are too busy scab-picking."

When she learned that I was dating a psychiatric resident (doctor in training) who often didn't follow through, which left me hurt and disappointed, she immediately accused me of "loving to suffer as well." Taken aback, I realized Alma was right. In many ways I was reenacting the same dysfunctional and hurtful relationship I had had with my father.

Though she appeared tough, there was a soft side to Alma. I saw how she was able to get close to every patient through patience and persistence. She understood that the traumas her patients had suffered early on when they had no control over their lives now led them to believe that their ongoing self-destructive patterns were also beyond their control. Alma taught me to be fearless in confronting those patients, and she taught me to be fearless in confronting myself. Victims are unable to change until they see that they are, in part, choosing to perpetuate unhelpful and self-destructive behaviors. Victims blame others, people who change look inward. The key is insight.

In developing Summer Search, I began to realize that we could not only provide access to transformational summer programs that give kids a chance to develop critical skills like self-efficacy, growth mindset, and agency, we could also be the kind of mentors that would challenge them to develop and grow through the reflection that allowed them to retell then rewrite their life narrative. We could be mentors like Mr. Langdon and Alma for me.

The first few years were all about experimentation. Gradually, I identified and then applied a few basic tools from my private practice to build successful mentoring relationships.

Four Basics of Successful Mentoring
Listen
Be patient. Take the time to get to know a person by putting yourself in his or her shoes.

Expand
Instead of giving advice and solutions to extremely complicated problems, get more information and listen. Truth is in the details of a story.

Question
Ask *why*—not to control or to fix, but to understand.

Wait
Slowly, carefully begin working together to look inward for insight.

To listen, expand, question, and then patiently wait is to give another person the unique opportunity to tell, retell, rethink, and then reconstruct their story. More simply, it gives them the gift of being heard and therefore feeling understood. For most of us, once we have that special opportunity to be heard without judgment, we are more likely to assume responsibility for ourselves instead of looking outside for a savior or someone to blame. *When we accept responsibility for ourselves, we stop resenting others.*

Insight mentoring does use some of the techniques of therapy— making the unconscious conscious, for example. Other elements are also similar: telling one's story, retelling through self-reflection, and rewriting through insight. However, in practice the two are quite different. By encouraging self-reflection and awareness through direct talk and action, Summer Search mentoring attempts to accelerate the learning process that is essential if mentor and student together are to start up the difficult pathway that leads out of victimhood and poverty.

That learning process, when combined with emotionally corrective experiences—two lengthy summer programs away from home—and weekly mentoring conversations, can change the trajectory of a life.

By the time Summer Search was in its sixth year, Jay had set up our first satellite office in Boston and the students there had all successfully completed their first trip. In San Francisco we had solid numbers: 100 percent of our students graduated from high school and 93 percent went on to college. In just a few years, the data would show that 89 percent of our students would graduate from college. Students from comparable economic groups overall have a college graduation rate of 11 percent.[2]

When I first started Summer Search, people often insisted that it was a mistake to give full scholarships. If students didn't take on a portion of the cost, the reasoning went, they would not value the opportunities. I discovered that the opposite was true. Covering everything, footing the whole bill, created such a level of gratitude that we were able to demand a significant return on our investment. Every Summer Search student is expected to:

Begin
Speak honestly and take a risk in their initial interview, go off alone, and do their best to persevere through the inevitable challenges and struggles of their first summer program.

---

2. Engle, Jennifer and Vincent Tinto. *Moving Beyond Access: College Success for Low-Income, First-Generation Students.* Washington D.C.: Pell Institute for the Study of Opportunity in Higher Education. 2008.

Believe

Develop their voice through weekly calls with their mentor, work on essay writing and public speaking skills, and put those skills into action.

Become

Transcend the handicaps of their backgrounds and become role models and future leaders.

These expectations are huge. They also indicate to every student that we believe it is possible with hard work, persistent effort, and courage for them to change the fundamental circumstances of their lives. In order for them to do that, they must *go for hard*. Make the hard choices, move *toward* rather than away from challenge and discomfort. In essence, this is asking adolescents to increase their self-efficacy and maintain a growth mindset. To believe that no matter how high the mountain, they can climb it. We support them every step and when they reach the top, we will be there to celebrate that victory with them.

Summer Search mentoring also changes the power dynamic. Almost all adolescents perceive relationships with parents, teachers, policemen, relatives, and other authority figures as variations on the parent-child relationship. Parents and other authority figures have the power, and they do not. Adolescents struggle with this dynamic by reacting in one of two ways: pleasing or rebelling. Most adolescents bounce from one to the other and some may even try for both at the same time!

Successful mentoring bypasses this battle and creates a unique adult-adult relationship where both parties agree to work together as equals to achieve agreed-upon goals. For example, in a relationship with a parent or teacher, an adolescent might confide they are smoking marijuana every weekend. This is cause for alarm; consequences are called for. In the Summer Search mentoring relationship, another dynamic emerges. The mentor listens. Only when she or he has all the details does the mentor begin to explore with the student the pros and cons of this behavior. In the absence of an unequal power dynamic, the student doesn't fear judgment (as much) and can talk more freely and honestly.

And while a parent-child relationship necessarily centers on rewarding, punishing, and controlling behaviors, the adult-adult relationship is based on *understanding* behaviors. This means having the patience and interest to listen longer, take in all the details, and finally, slowly, to ask the student to look inward for the answers. Adolescents are constantly trying to understand their own complicated selves during a period of development where intense turmoil is normal. Yet it is critical to remember, while the mentor can be an excellent sounding board, act as a steady guide; it's the student who must discover her or his own answers.

It is also important for mentors to remember that all adolescents act out, behave impulsively, and make mistakes—on an occasional, or even a regular basis. That's how they discover and develop their identities. It's also how their brains are wired. Temple University psychologist Laurence Steinberg, a leading thinker on adolescent brain science, has discovered that teenagers use different parts of their brains than adults to process what they are feeling.[3] Teenagers use the amygdala, a small, almond-shaped region that guides instinctual or "gut" reactions, while adults rely on the prefrontal cortex, which governs reason, self-regulation, and planning. As teens get older, the limbic system and the prefrontal cortex become more connected.

---

3. Steinberg, Laurence. "How Adolescents Think." Lessons from the *New Science of Adolescence*. New York: Eamon Dolan, Houghton Mifflin Harcourt, 2014. 70–71.

But during the teenage years, adolescents are dependent on a less mature part of the brain that makes them prone to impulsiveness and risk-taking.

Summer Search students have the additional burden of growing up in poverty. Most of them have experienced highly stressed and therefore often erratic parenting. Continuity—calling a mentor once a week, for example—is often an alien concept. Even the idea that someone has the time to just listen can be disconcerting.

When teenagers don't follow through—for example, in the case of Summer Search, if they don't call in once a week, or if they miss an appointment, or fail to participate in required activities—they often fall back on two very familiar refrains: "It's not my fault," and the ever comfortable, "I guess I'm just a procrastinator." The students initially expect their mentors to engage them in discussions about fault, blame, or lack of blame, or maybe try and fix the problem: suggesting they write things down and counseling them on time-management techniques. In short, they expect their mentors to revert to the parent-child power dynamic as the other authority figures in their life usually do.

By avoiding that type of discussion, Summer Search mentoring initially pulls the rug out from under students. It's not about the "rules," it's about something else: insight. This kind of mentoring is both time-consuming and threatening because it demands something that's challenging for most young people: self-analysis. "Going deeper," the mentor calls it in early conversations with the puzzled and often frightened students. Yet, as mentor and student start to understand this process, they slowly begin to experience the unique freedoms of the examined life. John Murray, a Summer Search board member in the San Francisco office, described insight-oriented mentoring succinctly: "*Other programs prepare the path for the student; Summer Search prepares the student for the path.*"

But, of course, habits are hard for all of us to break. The same issues come up again and again—which is why the steady mentoring continues for three years of high school or, sometimes, as we were soon to learn, far beyond.

For students, participation in Summer Search is all about risk: the risk of telling their story in their initial interview; the risk of leaving, going off alone on a trip; the risk of coming home; and the ongoing exposure of retelling their story in weekly phone conversations with their mentor. Through this risk-taking, students become more resilient, more consistently higher-performing, and more altruistic— all of which propels them toward achieving long-term goals.

Today in education, there is a renewed interest in investing in more than just a student's cognitive learning skills—and this is true for affluent as well as for disadvantaged children. Whether it's character development in Paul Tough's book *How Children Succeed*, Madeline Levine's coping skills in *Teach Your Child Well*, or Gerald Chertavian's insistence on learning practical skills (like how to dress and speak appropriately and be on time) in *Year Up*,[4] there is a burgeoning understanding that it's important to identify and develop the skills and underlying values that make for a more satisfying as well as a more successful life. On closer inspection, the words used to describe character and values in all of these books begin to dovetail and overlap. Tough's book identifies seven: grit (the most talked about), self-control, zest, social intelligence, gratitude, optimism, and curiosity. Levine's seven are: resourcefulness, enthusiasm, creativity, a good work ethic, self-control, self-esteem, and self-efficacy. Chertavian writes about honesty and tenacity. Another program, CASEL, the

---

4. Tough, Paul. *How Children Succeed: Grit, Curiosity, and the Hidden Power of Character*. Houghton, Mifflin, Harcourt, 2012; Levine, Madeline, *Teach Your Children Well: Parenting for Authentic Success*. New York: Harper, 2012; Chertavian, Gerald, *A Year Up: How a Pioneering Program That Teaches Young Adults Real Skills for Real Jobs with Real Success*. New York: Viking. 2012.

Callaborative for Academic, Social and Emotional Learning, led by researcher and psychologist Roger Weissberg, defines the core competencies of social and emotional learning or SEL, as self-awareness, self-management, social-awareness, relationship skills, and responsible decision making.[5]

What undergirds them all is developing social and emotional skills that will lead to better prospects. Whether it's about grit or self-discipline, it means *going for hard.*

Insight Mentoring is designed to also help young people develop specific life skills. Listed below, these skills also include quotes from different Summer Search students:

Tell Your Story

Again and again, Summer Search students refer to their initial interview—that moment when they "spilled the beans," often for the first time—as life-altering. When students choose to take the risk of being themselves and telling their story when they discover they are accepted for that choice, that realization becomes transformational.

> In my sophomore year of high school, I was nominated for Summer Search. I didn't really understand what it was about, and I didn't care because I was certain I would not be accepted. Since I was inevitably going to be rejected, I decided to reject them first. I was vague and kept looking away, but this annoying woman kept saying, "Look me in the eye." To my amazement, they were not fazed by my non-compliance. I began to tell my story. —Jessica

Wisdom through Telling and Retelling the Story

Learning the skill of telling and retelling our story brings a new perspective that can lead to wisdom. As we become more adept and

---

5. www.easel.org.

authentic in reaching out to others, we also become more successful in developing future personal and professional relationships. For Summer Search students, the lengthy process of talking weekly to mentors teaches them that their story is important, their voice is uniquely their own, and that they are valuable.

> Summer Search was challenging from the start. I had never been able to bring myself to tell anyone about the things that have hurt me deep inside, let alone strangers, but that would have to change. In the phone calls I dug deep to tell those painful memories buried in my heart. The memories I had of losing multiple family members along with people disappearing for no reason at all. I hated every moment of it, but I quickly realized that every time I revealed something I kept hidden, I felt a little bit better each time. — Jahil

Complete a Challenging Summer Program

The first trip, almost always a wilderness expedition, is challenging for every student. No student was more descriptive of this reality than the following young woman.

> The summer of my sophomore year, I was the lucky recipient of a Summer Search scholarship. I went to what I can only describe as a "survival camp" in Central Quebec. To this day, I wonder how I managed to handle waking up at 5:00 in the morning with eyes swollen from mosquito bites to put on frozen socks and shoes that rubbed the skin off my feet and canoe nine hours a day. We paddled less than 50 miles upstream, but we had to portage our equipment through swamps and clouds of blood-sucking flies. To quit or complain was not an option. We all knew we had to go on.
>
> Not a word was uttered when I wedged my ankle between two rocks and scraped off all the flesh, or even when we waded in through swampy water full of bloodsucking leeches. This time in my life, I refer to as five weeks in hell, but I loved every minute of it. That doesn't mean that I ever want to do it again, though.
>
> Sitting in the canoe, fighting the waves, I had all this time to think about the world I left behind. My grandmother had passed away, and I didn't let myself feel anything

or even say good-bye. But on the trip I would cry and cry, thinking about her. This trip broke me up physically, and gradually I started to let out emotions I had held inside so many years. Once I yelled at my leader, which scared me because I had never yelled at anyone my whole life.

There were only 10 of us with two leaders. At first we talked a lot, but as the trip wore on, we said less and less. I began to know what my tentmate was thinking. We communicated our feelings through looks and touch because speaking out loud caused that extra effort, and we were beyond exhaustion. We were out and we were part of it all, and eventually there were no words to describe it.

The last few days of the trip, we passed through camps with enormous piles of goose feathers where hunters had cleaned their trophies. There were the remains of a dead moose, shot and left in the bush because it was too heavy for the motorboats to carry. We all felt so violated. I wondered how our Cree Indian guide felt. He had been leading expeditions into the wild for 20 years, and every time the end of the forest came closer and closer. The sounds of bulldozers would get louder until they would drown out the distant cry of the hawk and white-throated sparrow. As we canoed under that last towering iron logging bridge, we saw the world of wolves and ancient forests, which we had been born into and almost forgotten, slip away.

Shock after shock hit me, bright fluorescent lighting, not being able to see the horizon, the smell of underarm deodorant and artificial perfumes. But the biggest shock of all was my reflection. I just stood there in front of the mirror watching an image move with me. I lifted up my hand and saw dirt ingrained into every crevice. The hand was attached to a tan, strong, muscular arm, which rose with mine. A person scarred with bug bites, who had a sun-baked face, stared straight back into my eyes. She was wearing my faded and torn blue T-shirt. I fell backward on the bathroom wall in total shock. It took about 10 minutes to realize it was me. — Mical

Not all of the wilderness expeditions have this level of adversity, but each one does offer some degree of difficulty: the challenge of going off alone to join a group of strangers, the challenge of doing something alien, the challenge of prolonged physical discomfort and exertion, and for Summer Search students often the challenge of being the only scholarship student. Many of the wilderness expeditions include a solo of one to three days and the chance for deep reflection. For students who persist and complete their summer programs, there is a significant sense of accomplishment, an increase in self-efficacy, and agency. As Jabali put it, "I have been to the top of the mountain. I can do anything!"

To Embrace Anger

Anger fed is soon dead, tis starving that makes it fat.

—Emily Dickinson

Anger is a scary emotion for most of us. Young people who are trying to achieve often keep rigid control over their own impulses and deny negative emotions. For inner-city students, acting out anger creates the potential for getting hurt in their neighborhoods and can be a threat to fragile relationships at home. In my psychiatric training, I was taught that suppressing anger makes students vulnerable to depression. Today, that early psychoanalytic thinking is considered outmoded by many clinicians. Cognitive behavioral approaches do not factor in suppressed anger in treating depression, and pharmacological approaches rely on medication. Yet in 20 years of private practice I have repeatedly seen patients relieved of the burden of sadness when given the permission to appropriately vent anger and frustration. The same is true for Summer Search students. They consistently feel better when their mentors help them talk about rather than swallow their frustrations.

Research shows that when young people learn to express, understand, and regulate their emotions they have better academic and social outcomes. Yet most children are never taught to recognize, let alone express their emotions in healthy ways. Marc Brackett, Director of the Yale Center for Emotional Intelligence, developed an approach to social and emotional learning, called RULER, that gives kids the opportunity to learn to regulate their own emotions and understand the perspectives of others.[6] RULER is a critical skill because suppressed emotions demand expression. For Summer Search students, this often happens after they return home from the first trip, confident and transformed—only to be confronted with the same overwhelming problems.

Yet expressing anger safely can be problematic. Mentors can act as the spout on the tea kettle that gradually lets off steam. By absorbing and validating their students' frustrations, they help them see that their anger is valid. This is not as hard as it sounds; it may simply involve closely listening while supporting their students' emotions: "I hear you. You did the right thing. I'm proud of you for letting these feelings out here in safe ways. You deserve to be mad. We will talk again next week but for now, right on."

Reject the Victim Mentality

Many young people growing up in poverty struggle at times with feeling like victims. In truth, they are often victimized, living in dangerous neighborhoods with highly stressed and single parent families while being confronted with the other harsh realities of poverty. The challenge for every student is to separate the experience of having literally been a victim (something students have no control over) from developing a victim mentality (a choice students can control).

---

6. Yale Center for Emotional Intelligence

When I was seven, my father left my mother and me in that trailer park. He was an alcoholic who showed up to visit once a month if I was lucky. I had bad luck. He died three years later. When he left, my mom fell apart and turned to alcohol as well as the emotional abuse of me; she was the earliest and closest example I had of how to be a victim. For her...life was a big conspiracy, everyone was out to get her. All her failures, faults, and shortcomings had nothing to do with the bad choices she made. She could not take the blame for anything, and because she viewed her mistakes as a function of the actions of others, she could not change and achieve anything substantial. This lifestyle sadly is not isolated to impoverished single mothers: it is found in people from all walks of life, and it is also part of me. —Jessica

Learn to Listen

The willingness to listen is a direct reflection of how much we value each other. Talking—more specifically, being listened to—reduces stress, and students coming from the deprivations, violence, and chaos of poverty are almost always highly stressed. A study by Michael Meaney about baby rats and their mothers demonstrated that baby rats whose mothers soothe them when they're frightened by licking and grooming grow up to be more curious, more confident, and less aggressive as adults. They even live longer.[7] Obviously, rats and kids are different—but both surely benefit from being nurtured. It's not licking, but silently, actively listening to someone without interrupting, that serves that nurturing function for humans. And nothing teaches young people more about how to become good listeners than having a mentor who consistently and intently listens to them. The ability to listen with intention and compassion creates and enhances qualities like curiosity, empathy, and altruism.

---

7. Meaney, Michael S. "Maternal care, gene expression, and the transmission of individual differences in stress reactivity across generations." *Annual Review of Neuroscience*, 24 (2001): 116–1192.

Respect Parents

Parenting is challenging for everyone. Parents in poverty, parents in crisis, and parents who have been dislocated and suffered as immigrants face special challenges. No matter how dysfunctional, abusive, or neglectful a parent seems to be, that parent still fills that essential, symbolic role for their child and is the only parent or adoptive parent that child will ever have. The more I have listened to adolescents tell often painful stories about their parents, the more I learned not to be negative or critical. Instead, the best way to empower students is to help them understand why their parents act the way they do.

> Shakespeare said it is a wise father who knows his own child, but I think it is a wise child who knows his own father. I listen to stories of my father's past growing up in Ukraine and how much harder it was for him. His family was so poor that during the winter he had to wear his sister's stockings under his summer shorts to keep warm, and he'd get beaten up at school for it. —Igor

It's Okay to Not Be Like Your Parent

Mentors can help students learn to empathize with their parents and caretakers but at the same time understand that it is not a betrayal if they create their own path. They do not have to perpetuate what are often generation-spanning patterns of destructive behaviors.

> As the interview progressed, I slowly opened up, and I remember, most vividly, saying, "I do not want to be like my mom. I do not want the adversity and hardships I have faced to define me. I want to create my own successes, victories, and even defeats, and for them to make up who I am. —Jessica

Understand Why Success Is Scary

For most students who live in poverty, success (this usually but not always means going to college) is a distant hope, a dream, a foreign possibility. Mentors can help students understand that success, although longed for, is often unconsciously more uncomfortable than failure, which is at least familiar for students from low-income communities, where statistically very few are able to break the cycle of poverty. Success can also be a threat to fragile relationships, which explains why so many students pull back and undo their hard-won successes.

> No one in my family graduated high school. I was the next one to either make a new path and graduate or follow my sisters down a familiar road. Here is where I found myself at a crossroads. If I followed my sisters I would not be alone, I would have them guide me through their same decisions. The ones that hurt my mom. As much as I wanted to graduate, I told myself success was too unknown and too scary. The same role models who taught me my basics, tying my shoes, A-B-Cs and 1-2-3s, failed. How could I succeed? — Jesus

Understand and Manage Stress

One of the most important things a mentor can do to empower students to succeed is to help them understand the role that stress plays in their lives and the difference between healthy and unhealthy outlets. Children who grow up in the instability that comes with poverty lead highly stressful lives. The part of the brain most impacted by stress is the prefrontal cortex—the same part that helps them develop emotional and cognitive self-regulatory abilities. This is one reason why highly stressed children have trouble self-regulating, focusing, following directions—even sitting still. One research study led by University of Pennsylvania researcher Angela Duckworth documents that the effects of stress and negative life events has a direct impact on adolescents' ability to self-regulate, control their impulses, and resist temptations to not persist toward long-term goals.[8] In another study Head Start teachers report that more than 25

---

8. Duckworth, Angela L., Betty Kim and Eli Tsukayamia. "Life Stress Impairs Self-Control in Early Adolescence." *Frontiers in Psychology* 2, 2012: 608.

percent of their students demonstrate seriously negative self-control behaviors.[9]

Unhealthy outlets include: withdrawing and bottling up feelings, cutting, overeating or restricting food, violent behavior, relying on passive activities like TV and video games, alcohol and drug use, premature sexual activity, and blaming others.

Healthy outlets for stress include: exercise, talking, creative pursuits, crying, and in venting anger safely through words and exercise in safe environments.

Considering the significant physical and emotional impacts of stress and the need for healthy outlets, the Summer Search expectation that students call weekly and exercise daily takes on a new perspective. Calling in is not about mindlessly complying with a rule, and exercising is not about losing weight. Talking and exercising reduce anxiety. Reducing anxiety decreases the destructive role that stress plays on the prefrontal cortex and increases concentration. Concentrating helps performance in school and promotes a feeling of well-being.

Value Humor

Adolescents are allergic to sarcasm from adults, but almost always respond well to humor. When a mentor and a student can start poking fun with each other, the friendly teasing becomes a vehicle for developing an even closer and more trusting relationship. Learning to laugh at oneself is an important life skill for us all.

> I was sitting in my interview in school with three strange ladies with Botox faces that never cracked a smile. There was nothing to do but tell them my story. —Carlos

---

9. Janis B. Kupersmidt, Donna Bryant, and Michael T. Willoughby. "Prevalence of Aggressive Behaviors Among Preshoolers in Head Start and Community Child Care Programs." *Behavioral Disorders* 26, No. 1 (November 2000).

Mistake-Making Is Essential

Everyone makes bad choices. Indeed, almost everyone will argue that making mistakes is an important part of developing character. A remarkably small number (2 to 3 percent) of Summer Search students do not complete their summer trips—despite the fact that these experiences are challenging in the extreme. When that happens it is essential that the mistake-maker experiences true remorse. Students *need* to feel badly about the mistakes they make and to understand the consequences. For example, in Summer Search, when a student loses heart and quits early, she or he must go beyond blame (bad kids, bad leader) and beyond excuses ("It wasn't my fault, it was too hot") to understand how their decision affects others—their group members and the program that offered the scholarship. We guarantee students will complete their trips, and when one doesn't, a possible outcome is the loss of a scholarship for a new student the following year. Most importantly, regret and remorse are the first steps in turning a mistake into a growth opportunity. With this kind of mentoring, students develop a growth mindset and believe that success is about learning, and that they can change over time by embracing challenges and the inevitable mistakes that come with them. Ironically, students who develop the courage and desire to take the risk of not performing well or perfectly, end up having better outcomes over time than those who are too afraid to risk failure.[10] We tell students, "It's not the mistakes you make in life—we all make them—it's how you handle them that counts."

The Value of the Examined Life

Insight mentoring, initially frightening to all of us, in time, helps most students develop an active and universal appreciation for

---

10. Dweck, Carol. "Inside the Mindsets" and "The Truth About Ability and Accomplishment." *In Mindset*, 15–81.

introspection. With greater self-understanding comes a greater desire to understand others. As I reflect on the skills and attitudes we cultivate in Summer Search students, I wonder what we would look like as a nation if we could develop those skills and attitudes in all young people. Perhaps as parents, educators, and youth leadership organizations, we should spend less time, energy, and resources preparing the path for the child, and focus instead on *preparing the child for the path.*

God made man because he loved stories

—Elie Wiesel

The following stories began in the early '90s as I was developing Summer Search, reaching out and getting to know adolescents who grew up much differently than I had. Young people who lived in the Acorn Projects of West Oakland and in the Sunnydale Projects of San Francisco, who struggled with social issues like being undocumented, severely learning disabled, and in foster care.

In those early unproven days, Solaria, Myra, David, and Levar were brave enough to put their trust in me as they learned to tell, retell, and then rewrite their stories. Those relationships began long before I learned how to teach others, long before I developed insight mentoring methods, and if truth be told, long before I knew what I was doing.

These students are the heroes of Summer Search, and their stories come with a perspective of a relationship that has lasted for over two decades, a relationship that is now a friendship that will last forever.

There were the times when none of us knew what to do—we figured it out together.

| six |

Indomitable: Solaria

Resilience reflects that which characterizes a twig with a fresh, green living core. When stepped on, such a twig bends, and yet springs back.
—George Vaillant

It took almost three years to find a cohort of outstanding teachers at high-risk schools throughout the Bay Area who were willing to volunteer precious time to identify students. Jan Hudson, the college counselor at Woodrow Wilson, was one of those rare individuals.

Wilson was a troubled high school in San Francisco that served kids from Bayview Hunters Point and Visitacion Valley, an area which included the Sunnydale Projects. The school, an even mix of African American, Latino, and Asian students with one or two Caucasians, consistently had the lowest math and reading scores in the entire city.

My first order of business: to find the gated teachers' parking lot. Once inside the school, the halls were crowded. As I made my way through pushing, swearing, and shouting students, they seemed not to notice there was an adult in their midst. It was a challenge to not bump into anyone.

The counseling center, a large room with brightly colored posters on the walls, was a welcome relief. Jan, an attractive woman about my age with rings on every finger and a colorful serape that looked hand woven, was waiting with six students who looked frightened. In a small side room, Jan prepped me for the day, giving me the schedule and some specific information about each student. She looked at me curiously. "We just met, but I'm wondering. What made you start a program like this?"

Caught off guard, I hesitated before saying, "I'm not sure." An image came to mind of three confused little girls standing barefoot in the muddy field listening to the dreaded words. Three little girls standing barefoot in a muddy field, confused. Our father was yelling, *Don't stand there like goddamned dummies!* We didn't know what he wanted. Finally he shouted, *Shut the gate, the horses will get out!*

Jan was waiting for a response. "I didn't have many opportunities growing up," I answered. She was about to ask another question, but the first student, Solaria, opened the door and started to come into the room. Jan told her to go back outside, then glanced over her shoulder. "I want you to interview that girl," she told me, "because although she is high-achieving, I'm sure she's involved in gangs." Her voice dropped to a whisper. "She's Mexican American and she may be undocumented."

Undocumented? That word, one I was unfamiliar with at the time, just one year later would take center stage in state politics and become an issue on everyone's mind. Illegal immigration led to Proposition 187, an emotional and controversial bill dubbed "Save Our State" by its supporters, appearing on the ballot. The proposition, which aimed to block access to social services and education to illegal immigrants, including roughly

308,000 children,[1] passed. Three days later, a judge ruled the law unconstitutional.

Yet at that moment, I was unaware of what the term "undocumented" meant or how pressing and explosive this issue would become. Before I could ask Jan to explain, Solaria, a petite girl with dark eyes heavily emphasized by black eyeliner, opened the door again, obviously nervous about her interview. Jan left, and the young woman sat down without being asked.

We stared at each other for a few seconds as she flipped back long, eggplant colored hair, teased high in front. "How are you today?" she asked. She had a pleasant voice, but her face was expressionless.

Knowing how small talk can derail the intensity of the interview, I frowned and didn't answer. She smiled and began talking about herself, focusing on her achievements. Her grades were excellent; she was the junior class representative to the Board of Education and president of the Latino Club. After talking about her activities specifically and at length, she finally paused.

I jumped in. "Your name is Solaria, right?"

She nodded and looked at me, then her gaze slid away. She flashed another smile, but for some reason it felt insincere. It was as if the young woman sitting right in front of me was actually watching and waiting from a distance.

"Tell me about your family."

"I forgot, I am in the Science Club too. My family? They're fine." Solaria crossed her arms across her chest. "I have two sisters and, of course, my parents. They work all the time." She paused. "That's it."

I wondered if Solaria was so guarded because she had heard about the personal nature of the interview. Almost 15 minutes had already

---

1. Margolis, Jeffrey Q. "Closing the Door to the Hand of Opportunity: The Constitutional Controversy Surrounding Proposition 187." The University of Miami, *Inter-American Law Review*, Vol. 26, No. 22 (1994–1995): 363–401.

passed, and she had managed to avoid talking about any of the harsh realities in her life.

I was quiet. In an attempt to keep the conversation going, she added that she had spent the last two weekends volunteering to register people to vote.

I was impressed. Not only was this young woman an accomplished leader with high grades, but her volunteer activities were unusual for a 15-year-old. I doubted that community service hours were a requirement at Wilson. But if she was going to be a candidate for Summer Search, she was going to have to take some risks and talk about herself more openly. Whatever program we chose would ask the same thing of her. The time to start was now.

The silence lengthened. With flushed face she said, "I don't know what else to say."

"What about the rest?"

"What do you mean?"

"Stuff other than your achievements."

"All I have are my achievements. I don't have anything else." The heavy eyeliner seemed to slide a bit, and I saw she was getting tearful. A long black streak began to roll down her cheek. The vulnerability she was trying so hard to hide was beginning to break through. But why was she so careful? What needed protecting?

It was time for me to take a risk. "What about your involvement in gangs?"

"Who told you about that?"

Silence.

"Oh. Well, actually, I did get arrested," she admitted with great delicacy. "Someone threw a gun in the car I was riding in. But the gun, it wasn't mine." I waited. After staring at me for a few more seconds, she pulled up her sweater sleeve. On her lower arm was a small round scar. "This happened in eighth grade. A girl from the projects just walked up and burned me with her cigarette." She paused and looked me straight in the eye. "You have to be part of something to get by here…you know?"

I started to tear up and closed my eyes for a brief second, then looked directly at Solaria. I did know. In the deprived and neglected area of the city that Wilson served, the kids from the Sunnydale Projects were bound to act out their anger at school. Solaria, who had tried to be so in control throughout the interview, now looked young and vulnerable. Still, I sensed there was something else, something she was evading, something still left unsaid. Yet I didn't know what to do.

It had hardly been a perfect interview, but this young woman was obviously talented and smart. She was a high-achieving Latina in a very low-performing school; with some good college counseling, she could be a candidate for a full scholarship to a private college. An academic experience on a college campus or at a boarding school could help prepare her for that opportunity. The director at Cornell Summer College had recently told me that she wanted more Latino students, as they were underrepresented in the program.

For 50 years Cornell University had offered high-performing high school juniors the chance to get a taste of college life in the summer. Students were told that the courses were fast-paced and more difficult than high school or AP classes. Since most participants come from private schools, it would be a stretch for a student from a school like Wilson to integrate and grasp the advanced academics.

"How about going to Cornell University this summer?"

"I don't know. Maybe. Where is it?"

"New York State. It's an Ivy League school." Solaria's eyes widened and she began to frown. I could also tell she didn't know what "Ivy League" meant but was too proud to ask. Well, she would soon find out.

I handed her a colorful brochure that described the range of classes on one of the most beautiful college campuses in the world. Solaria opened it and started to read. I patted her hand and told her to call me within a week. Startled that the interview was over so soon, she pulled out a mirror and glanced at her face. It was covered with black streaks. She jumped up, wiped her face, and left without saying good-bye. I sat alone waiting for the next student, wondering about the complicated issue of gang activity and how it played out in that young girl's life. Wondering also what was missing.

Later, just before she left for the East Coast, Solaria called and told me how confusing that interview had been for her. "I just couldn't imagine getting away, getting out of where I was, but I wanted it so bad. So when I told you about the gang stuff I was sure that it was all over. I had blown it; you would never offer me anything. When you asked me what I had learned about myself I didn't know what to do, what to say. All I could think about was why would anyone ever support a person who joined a gang?"

During the post-interview process, Solaria followed through on everything. She filled out the paperwork for her trip fairly quickly and booked her flight. Her mother was concerned about the plane ride to the East Coast because Solaria didn't have a driver's license, but I reassured her that a student photo ID card from school would suffice.

But Solaria's return was puzzling. I knew she had completed her trip and had made it back home, but she didn't check in for several weeks or return my calls. When she did finally call, late one afternoon, she had a lot to say.

"It was amazing, Linda. The academics were really hard. I pulled several all-nighters, but I did it! I also jumped into social life right away. At Wilson it's academics or the streets—where life has to do

with survival. My friends were part of the streets, so I always kept the two very separate. At Cornell those two things blended together."

Solaria's voice softened. "I could relax there in a whole new way. I didn't have to worry about protecting my back. No one was going to shoot at me or jump on me. There were 10 of us, and we studied together and went to the cafeteria together, sort of like our own little gang. It was weird to have my academics and my social life be the same. But it was hard. Those kids were smart. I struggled."

She paused then continued, "One day I saw an opening. The professor wanted someone to prepare a debate on a medical ethics issue. No one volunteered, so I raised my hand. At the end of the six-week session I won that debate in front of the whole student body. After that I wasn't an outsider anymore. I was inside. It was me inside, part of the Ivy League."

As Solaria described these successes, I was so happy for her—yet I also couldn't help but wonder why she had delayed so long in calling. This had been her first step away from her family, her first trip on an airplane, and her first time in a classroom with students from vastly different backgrounds. She had covered so much terrain, broken so many barriers; it must have taken a great deal of internal strength.

I could understand those achievements from my own experiences. After graduating nurses training in Indianapolis at 21 I wanted to move to California. The only way I could afford to do that was take the Greyhound bus. Arriving at the St. Louis bus station at 3:00 AM was a pretty scary proposition—I pressed on but all I really wanted to do was go home.

For Solaria, after all the risks she had taken, the opportunities ahead were going to be huge; I imagined a full scholarship to Cornell. When I suggested this, she reacted coldly: "I can't go to college."

"What are you talking about, Solaria? Of course you can go to college. You belong in college."

"I don't have papers."

"What does that mean?"

"I'm undocumented."

Silence. I didn't know what to say. Jan Hudson's whispered remark—"I think she's undocumented"—came back to me now. It was unconscionable. I had simply forgotten. My entire understanding of this girl, of this situation, was wrong and had been wrong from the very beginning. Why hadn't I done my homework? Something twisted inside. I should have understood what it would mean to raise the hopes of someone who was without hope.

There was a long sigh as she began to explain. Solaria and her family had lived in the U.S. for six years. Her parents had come from Mexico on a visa, but the visa had expired. They were all living here illegally. As "illegal aliens," the family was relegated to very low-paying jobs. As for Solaria, she was locked out of educational opportunities; her future was in serious jeopardy. As she talked, her tone remained strangely neutral.

Solaria was waiting for a response, so I offered some vague reassurance—we would figure it out somehow. But what was there to be done? I soon found out that she could, indeed, be accepted to a private college or to any of the University of California schools. They were all eager for Latinas with her grades. But there was no possibility of getting federal financial aid. And within the University of California system, Solaria would not qualify as an in-state resident, so she'd need to pay out-of-state fees on top of tuition. (In 1998 this requirement would be waived at all University of California schools for undocumented students if they had attended high school in the U.S.)

For now the whole issue felt too unclear, too frightening to confront.

There were 87 students that third summer. They had all completed their programs and returned home safely. Now that the euphoria was fading, I could feel most of them starting to lose energy. Yes, they had a different sense of themselves, but they were back, faced with the same dangerous neighborhoods and sometimes resentment from their peers and even from family members who couldn't relate to their experiences or their new ideas. These realities all chipped away at their confidence and newfound strengths.

It was time for the annual Fall Event. I now needed a much larger space; luckily, Georganne Ferrier, the teacher who had helped me with referrals at Oakland High School, offered the use of the school's auditorium. Though overcrowded and occasionally dangerous, Oakland High, with its large gated parking lot, was a great place for an evening gathering.

I decided to ask a Vietnamese Summer Search student, Uyen Nguyen (pronounced "Win Win"), to be the master of ceremonies. The speakers included an East Indian athlete who would speak about the pressure to stay home, chastely covered (instead of running around soccer fields in shorts), and a Caucasian boy from a suburban school describing his family's experience with bankruptcy.

An interesting lineup—but what about Solaria? Although she couldn't speak publicly about her illegal status, her story could show others how leadership abilities can get diverted into gang activity when there are no other outlets. And I was curious. Would she agree to talk more honestly and specifically about what it was like to be in a gang? On impulse, I asked her about speaking. After a prolonged silence, she said she didn't remember those parts of her history. I pushed her, and she admitted that, yes, of course she remembered, but it was too personal. After another long silence she agreed.

Organizing an event and dinner for several hundred people seemed easy compared to the job of preparing four students to give speeches. Week after week, I listened to them practice and, gradually, each one got stronger and clearer. Solaria was the exception. In spite of my coaching, she remained vague and ambivalent.

Dinner was potluck, which caused some consternation. The immigrant students called anxiously to ask what the word "casserole" meant. That night, brightly colored tablecloths were slowly dotted with platters of noodles, shrimp and rice dishes, enchiladas in all kinds of different sauces nestled among tubs of Kentucky Fried Chicken and supermarket pies.

The students began to congregate. Guests included mothers, grandmothers, a few fathers, a sprinkling of aunts and uncles, foster parents, teachers, and the few Summer Search donors who were adventurous enough to come to an inner-city high school at night.

After eating, everyone went into the crowded auditorium to hear the student testimonials. Uyen began with a warm welcome and a short story about his challenges on his trip to France run by an East Coast boarding school. The other students were all from private schools and knew how to speak French. Uyen had never heard of the books they had read. As the future valedictorian of his low-functioning public school in Oakland, he was initially intimidated, but by the end of the trip he won an award for most improved student. The East Indian young woman spoke about how it felt to be caught between two different cultures, and the white student how shameful it felt to lose his home. Each speech seemed to bring this disparate group closer together—there were "amen"s and "you got it, sister"s as the kids became emotional. The audience slowly began to feel like one family, one community.

The final speaker was Solaria, who began speaking immediately. "When I came for my interview with Linda, I was different. My hair was teased high, I was wearing lots of makeup, and I had…a big attitude. But Linda didn't know it, because I wasn't going to tell her anything." Solaria broke into a huge smile at the laughter from the audience.

This was nothing like what she had said in practice with me. After the laughter the audience grew silent as the crowd tried to reconcile that description with the poised young woman on the podium.

Solaria continued, "I started school at the Visitation Valley Middle School, where the math was about third-grade level, stuff I had already known for years in Mexico. I did not speak the language, and most of the kids were from a rough upbringing from the nearby Sunnydale Projects. One of them just walked up and burned my arm with a cigarette. By high school I was done with the bullying—I joined a gang."

Solaria looked intently at the audience. "I have never told anyone what being in a gang was like. How dangerous it was to simply ride alone on a bus. One day some strange girls began to get on, one at each stop. I moved up near the driver. When I jumped off, they followed. There were nine of them; they surrounded me." Solaria paused before continuing. "They beat me up and just left me lying on the sidewalk. After that, I vowed that no one would ever hurt me again. In spite of my small size, I became a successful street fighter. I took martial arts classes that I paid for with my babysitting money. All you really need to know is how to throw a punch, so I won tournaments and hid my trophies from my parents."

She paused again and looked around the audience. "I want to tell you a story. One day I went to my friend's house. She's only 15 and already she had a baby, a real pretty baby. As I held and admired this baby, she said, 'Do you want it?' *She wasn't kidding.* At that moment I realized that I could be like her before I had the chance to accomplish anything. I could even become like the rest of them; cold and hardened by the choices I was making.

"Then I had my Summer Search interview, the moment that changed everything. I was recognized for my ambition and strength in a different way. I was perceived as smart. So I went to the East Coast to an Ivy League school to study with some of the world's smartest kids. I didn't fail. When I came home from Cornell, my gang friends wanted me to come back. But I just said, 'I can't. I have a life.' And I did. I ran for president of the school and won."

The applause lasted a long time. As she sat down, Solaria glanced around the audience until she saw me. Our eyes locked. I nodded, and a nearly imperceptible smile crossed her face. She had taken the risk of exposing herself for me. This young woman was not going to become another hardened, low-income, pregnant teenager. She was going to get an education. Some day she would understand that she took this enormous risk, not just for me, but for herself.

It was time to find an immigration lawyer.

* * *

Solaria was going to graduate from high school the following year. Like other seniors, she needed to start getting ready for college—but unlike most of her peers, that next step would be impossible for her until she changed her immigration status. I had found a lawyer, David Brooks, who had agreed to see her at a reduced cost. But her family was afraid. By making that appointment and by starting that process, they risked deportation. I now understood why the issue was so delicate and why Solaria had been so vague and evasive. The need to function and excel, while simultaneously remaining invisible, had been the dominating reality of her life.

When the family finally met with the lawyer, he told them they had a chance. They had been in the U.S. for over six years and had worked steadily. But there was some risk. As a first step, they had to get letters—lots of letters—of recommendation. Her parents, after hesitating, took this step out of the shadows, at great risk, so Solaria and her two sisters could get an education. They got letters from their landlord, from their employers, and their friends, while the girls got letters from their teachers. I had a friend who knew Congresswoman Nancy Pelosi; an immigration expert in her office wrote a letter advocating for this hard-working family. The lawyer submitted the paperwork to the courts, and the family waited. Then they waited some more.

In February I was back at Woodrow Wilson to interview new students and to reconnect with seniors. Solaria was late for her interview—a surprise. When she came, she told me tearfully that Wilson was closing. It wasn't much of a school, but it was her school and she was the senior class president.

After giving me a cursory report about her meetings with the immigration lawyer, Solaria fell silent. There was no word on when they would get their court date, and there was no assurance that they would get green cards. In fact, there was a good chance that they would be deported. As for college, time was running out. I didn't know what to say or do. After a long pause, she told me her grades were still good, but it was hard to keep her focus.

It was essential to keep her hopeful. I said, "There has to be a solution. A Summer Search board member is interested in this whole issue, and I'll do some more research—I promise. Keep your grades and your spirits up, and we will develop a plan. I won't leave you hanging. Do you hear me?"

Solaria's face was flushed. We shared a quick hug as she left.

A few weeks later, Solaria's counselor, Jan Hudson, sent me a newsletter from an East Coast boarding school called Northfield Mount Hermon. It had a long article about their GAP year program. The school granted full scholarships to high-potential minority youth for a fifth year of high school. This new possibility intrigued me. A fifth year of high school would buy Solaria time, as well as give her the chance to compensate for some of her educational deficits. Even top students at Wilson didn't have access to the basics—especially in writing—and as Solaria had pointed out, her middle school math courses had lagged three years behind the material she had already studied in Mexico, and high school wasn't much better.

Solaria was surprised by the idea of another year of high school, but quickly realized the magnitude of the opportunity and mailed in an excellent application. The admissions director at Northfield Mount Hermon, a woman named Pam Shoemaker, recognized her talent, but was not sure the school could take an undocumented student. It seemed that no one was willing to grapple with this complicated issue. A few days later, Pam called to tell me that Solaria would receive a full $25,000 scholarship. In the fall of 1994—the year Prop 187 passed—she was going to get a private-school education.

I scheduled a lunch with Sally Hambrecht, the founding board member who had expressed interest in undocumented students. Sally, whose grandson had gone to Northfield Mount Hermon, was pleased with the resolution to Solaria's dilemma. She asked if I would put the issue of kids without green cards on the agenda of the next board meeting.

Her suggestion was good, but it also reminded me of my tendency to act independently. Years of working alone in a private practice had not prepared me to be a team player. I had been running Summer Search for three years, guided by a kind and competent board of directors, but I hadn't asked enough of them. This was a skill I had yet to learn.

I also worried that the board members would think my actions had been rash. Yet knowledge expands awareness, and I was at last aware of the public cost of not allowing high-achieving Latino students the opportunity for a college education, especially with changing demographics in the U.S. Latinos are the fastest growing minority group. According to the Pew Research Center, by 2014, Latinos would replace Caucasians as California's largest ethnic group.[2]

At every Summer Search board meeting, a student speaks for the first 15 minutes. Solaria had just left for the East Coast, so I invited Lila, another undocumented student, to share her story. Reluctant at first, she agreed after I told her she was safe.

This meeting took place eight years before 9/11 and 12 years before President Obama announced his administration's plans to mend our nation's immigration policy. The centerpiece of those plans was called the Dream Act. The goal was to create access to college for high-achieving Latino youth who had been brought to this country illegally as young children. The Dream Act was narrowly defeated in September 2010. Today Congress is still debating the fate of 11 million people with a lack of urgency that is startling.

2. "In 2014, Latinos will surpass whites as largest racial/ethnic group in California." (Accessed July 20, 2104.) http://www.pewresearch.org/fact-tank/2014/01/24/in-2014-latinos-will-surpass-whites-as-largest-racialethnic-group-in-california/

I introduced Lila to the board and told them that I wanted them to understand some of the complexities around immigration issues for our undocumented students. Even though I had been acting independently, we all shared the responsibility for the decisions I was making.

Lila, the only Latina among Asian students in advanced placement classes at Oakland High School, began talking about her long journey as a baby from El Salvador to the U.S. A beautiful girl with long, curly black hair and an expressive face that radiated sincerity, she spoke clearly and simply. I could feel the board members becoming intrigued as she described how she loved math and wanted to become an engineer. Yet she couldn't even think of going to college.

Lila stopped talking mid-sentence. There was a long silence. I gave her a nod, and her face flushed. Then she said something she had never said before in public. She said out loud that she was an undocumented person. It was this terrible thing, this shameful and insurmountable barrier that kept her from fulfilling her hopes. Her voice shook and a large tear rolled down her cheek. Lila looked around the room anxiously, but no one moved or spoke. She began to sob.

Out of the corner of my eye, I saw Sally's face. Her hands shook as she waved them in the air, "Wait!"

Ten carefully composed faces turned slowly in her direction. Sally's hands continued shaking as she waved at the group.

"I don't understand."

There was dead silence.

"This is America!"

The other board members were startled but also moved by Lila's and Sally's emotional outburst. They began to nod as Sally continued. "I think that highly qualified students like Lila have the right to get an education."

Yet the room remained silent.

"I don't get it," Sally persisted. "Can Lila go to college if somebody pays? What if someone pays?"

"Yes," I answered. "She just can't apply for a Cal Grant or a Pell Grant. Someone will have to make up those funds."

Sally's gray eyes were hard to read. For a few more seconds—seconds that felt like hours—there was another heavy silence. Her eyes narrowed. "I think we can fix that problem."

After the meeting, I walked Lila to the bus stop. She looked at me, fear and hope simultaneously crossing her face. My voice was shaky as I tried to explain that we had just experienced a miracle or what the psychologist Carl Jung would call "synchronicity." Synchronicity is the simultaneous occurrence of events that appear to be significantly related but have no discernible causal connection. "What happened tonight, Lila, whatever we call it, is going to change your life."

Sally paid for Lila's college education and she graduated from the University of California in Los Angeles. She went on to marry a U.S. citizen and today is also a citizen as well as a mother and an engineer.

At the next board meeting, Sally Hambrecht turned to me. "Do you have another one?"

* * *

Despite what she described as a black cloud of doubt hanging over her head, Solaria did extremely well academically during her very challenging post-graduate year at Northfield Mount Hermon. She was admitted to almost all of the colleges she applied to, and was offered substantial financial aid packages. However, because she did not qualify for government aid and other scholarships available to low-income students, she was still locked out. Then Pam Shoemaker cleverly set up a personal interview for her with the admissions department at Brown University. After that, Brown somehow found the additional funds to accept her for a full scholarship for the first three years.

In the fall of her sophomore year at Brown, Solaria and her family finally got a court date for a hearing about their immigration status. "What's this about Brown University?" the judge murmured to herself. "My daughter applied to Brown. That's a very hard school to get into." Then, in a stunning instant, a family with no future became a family with a future of endless possibilities. They arrived at the hearing as illegal aliens and left as permanent residents on the pathway to citizenship.

This story recalls to mind the haunting words of Anne Michaels: "To survive was to escape fate. But if you escape your fate, whose life do you then step into?"

For Solaria the answer to that question was bold and definitive. She graduated from Brown University and worked in New York for several years. Then she applied and was accepted to Harvard Business School. Today, she is married to an HBS classmate, is a financial advisor at Morgan Stanley, and has participated as a board member in the new Summer Search office in the Silicon Valley.

seven

The Seeds of Empathy: David

What most people know
And school children soon learn
Those to whom evil is done
Do evil in return

—W.H. Auden

A boy who once described himself by saying he "didn't care nothing for nobody" was the one who enlarged my understanding of empathy. The word *empathy*, only a century old, derives from the same root as the word *pathos*, or suffering. In working with struggling young people through Summer Search, I began to wonder: is there a connection between suffering and empathy? I also began to wonder that about my own background. Why did the abuse I experienced growing up make me dream of becoming a nurse? Why does a harsh childhood lead some people to become empathetic, while others respond by hardening their hearts?

Science has proved that the same neural systems that become active when we are in pain also become activated when we experience the suffering of others. New research also indicates that the ability to feel empathy actually impacts heath even at a microscopic level. Steven Cole, a professor of medicine at UCLA has documented the fact that "our genes can tell the difference between a purpose-driven life and a shallower one even when our conscious minds cannot."[1]

The 15-year-old Vietnamese student who "cared nothing for nobody," was referred to Summer Search through someone who deeply believed in him: his counselor, Lettie Lupis. His name was David.

Lettie, a college counselor at one of the largest public schools in San Francisco, had an annual caseload of more than 600 students. We first met on an early spring morning in 1994. Her small airless office was so crowded with youngsters, surrounding her two chairs and cluttered desk, that almost everything else in the room was hidden from sight. A woman of substantial heft, Lettie was dressed in a bright turquoise pantsuit, set off by long, vividly painted fingernails. "It's called Watermelon Sunset, honey," she confided, when she caught me stealing a look.

Lettie began to talk at length about her determination to find opportunities for her high-risk students. There were hundreds of students whom she loved, and she was convinced I would accept all of them into the program. To my relief, although she had nominated 20 students, only eight had written the one-page essay required to qualify for an interview.

It was a Friday. I'd been interviewing students at different high schools all week. I was tired. Even eight seemed overwhelming—but

1. Reynolds, Gretchen, "Looking to Genes for the Secret to Happiness," *The New York Times Magazine.* August 23, 2013

arguing with this imposing woman wasn't an option. I got to work, interviewing students all morning in a small overheated room with no windows and continued straight through lunch. Then, somehow, it was 3:00 PM. David, the student who Lettie indicated was her top priority, was the last interview of the day. The door opened, and in walked a tall, athletic-looking Asian boy. Large diamond-like earrings glinted in both ears, and in spite of the warm room, he wore a handsome, expensive-looking black leather jacket and greeted me with an enormous grin.

I was tired and hungry, but I couldn't help smiling back at this animated boy. And when I did, his eyes gleamed even brighter. I was struck by his natural presence counterbalanced by a distinctively soft voice.

When I asked him what it was like to walk in his shoes, he began with energy but soon ran out of things to say. His mother worked all the time, and there were two younger sisters and a dad he didn't want to talk about. As for school, he didn't like it. Glancing at his transcript, I saw that he was failing most of his classes except for drama.

Before long, David's initial charm began to take on a sharper edge. The pressure of my personal questions—which required him not only to be present, but to reveal his inner life—was too much. He soon lapsed into one-word answers, bored shrugs, or impatient "I don't know"s. Only when he spoke about Miss Lupis did he give a more descriptive answer. "When I got in trouble at school, I didn't care. I didn't care nothing for nobody. They sent me to see Miss Lupis. You know, I was supposed to be punished or something, but she told me to sit down. Then she asked me if I was hungry. Lunch? I was confused. I was hungry, but I still wondered: why did she do that? So I walked out. She called out that she would get me some lunch the next day. It didn't make no sense to me. I just didn't care."

My own energy fading fast, I gathered my dwindling enthusiasm and said, "So, David, it sounds like you are interested in drama."

"Yeah, it's okay."

"I'll tell you something, David. This interview is just 'okay' too."

He stared at me sullenly. Gone was the bright shine in his eyes. "There ain't nuthin' more to tell."

I sighed. The eager boy who had walked in the door a half hour ago had faded from view, replaced by a person with slumped shoulders, poor English, spotty school attendance, dismal grades, and a big attitude. It all spelled trouble, but something stopped me from telling him he was not a candidate for the program. I sensed that, underneath his withdrawn and sulky performance, both in the interview and in school, he was smart. Until he shut down, he was quick, and in spite of language difficulties, he was an abstract thinker. Then there was the fact that Lettie was behind him. She knew him and his potential better than I did; he must have some redeeming qualities I couldn't quite see yet. To be fair, the interview was challenging. As a ninth-grader, David was younger than most students.

Summer Search was getting more structured. Students now almost always started in their sophomore year and participated in some kind of wilderness expedition that first summer. I gave them as much weekly mentoring as I could. A second formal interview in their junior year was followed by a more sophisticated summer program—often a family home stay or community service experience abroad.

David was young and high-risk. When I asked him what he had learned in his interview, he said he didn't know. With some trepidation, I handed him a brochure to a drama program which took kids throughout New England to perform improvisational skits in residential care facilities for seniors. It was a sweet and thoroughly unrealistic plan based on not nearly enough information. Lettie was thrilled.

Like many students do after a challenging interview, David didn't call back. In the beginning, this had perplexed me, but now, with four years' experience and some ongoing research, I was starting to understand why. Since a significant aspect of resiliency in adolescents is their ability to physically and psychologically *separate* from their parent or parents, in many ways, the selection process for participation in Summer Search was actually one of self-selection. So many students who are singled out by their teachers as "ones with potential," never go on to write the simple one-page essay to get an interview and so many also don't follow through after their interview. All students make these choices which give me room to take risks and see what happens.

In David's case, I felt relieved. His track record in school demonstrated he was not able to successfully participate in sustained activities. I also suspected that, once he got a real challenge on his summer program, he would probably drop out—just as he had during his interview. In spite of his superficial charm and my wish to see his potential—a potential that Lettie so believed in—he struck me as incapable of the most important quality I look for in all students: empathy. In addition to resiliency, I was learning that empathy was the most reliable indicator of a student's ability to grow and change. Not only was he incapable of empathy himself, he was puzzled by it in others.

A few weeks later, Lettie called and told me she forgot to mention that David was on probation for selling Chinese firecrackers. Probation? She also mentioned that David seemed to be falling apart. Just that morning, he had showed up at school drunk and was taken away by the police. She was worried. I felt for her, and for David too. At the same time, I was thankful. This boy was not

a candidate for Summer Search. For just a moment, those sparkling black eyes and that shining smile flashed through my mind. I pushed the image away.

A month later, when the phone rang, a vaguely familiar voice said, "Linda, it's me. I want to do a program."

"David?"

There was nervous laughter; this couldn't have been an easy call, but he was clearly pleased I recognized his voice. His mood quickly changed as I added, "Please don't waste my time."

"Come on, you know I'll follow through!"

"How could I possibly know that, David? You haven't been honest with me from the beginning, let alone come close to following through." Silence. Impulsively, I threw in, "Okay, if you can figure out a way to get to my office, I'll give you another chance. But don't come unless you want to talk with me about what's really going on."

Two hours and three buses later, David arrived. Looking at him closely, I wondered if he had ever been to the incredibly wealthy community of Mill Valley in Marin County where my husband and I had a small office. I noticed he was wearing another expensive-looking leather jacket, this time a brown one.

Before I could ask a question, David leaned forward in his chair and began talking—fast. "My mom left when I was little. My dad, like her, he was always working. There is just one bed in our apartment," he hesitated briefly, then continued with great intensity. "So at night I slept in the same bed with my dad and my three brothers. Since I was the youngest, I had to sleep at their feet."

He shot me a glance to see if I was following him before continuing. "They used to kick me all night long." He stopped abruptly and looked out the window. "I didn't know where my dad was most of the time. He didn't give me no money. There wasn't no food in the apartment."

"That sounds pretty tough."

David shot me another appraising look. "I grew up in the Tenderloin. Do you know where that is?"

I did. The San Francisco Tenderloin is located in the flatlands on the southern slope of Nob Hill, situated between the upscale shopping district of Union Square to the northeast and the stately Civic Center office district to the southwest. One of the few areas of the city to resist gentrification, it encompasses 50 square blocks. Violent street crimes like robbery and aggravated assault are especially prevalent. Graffiti and tagging are common, as is the use and sale of illicit drugs, which often occur in plain sight. A treacherous area for unsuspecting tourists and home to the poorest and most destitute people in the city, the image of David as a young boy threading his way through the chaos, the drunks, and the prostitutes made tears come to my eyes.

David, whose survival skills probably included reading people, noticed my eyes were tearing up. "You know it's hard, huh?" I nodded slowly. Reassured that he was understood and being heard, David continued more evenly. "It wasn't that bad, though, because the people in my neighborhood knew me, and sort of looked out for me. Later, I moved in with my mom in the Potrero Hill Projects. She has a restaurant, so my sisters and me, we hardly ever see her."

Once again, I understood that David was in another high-risk neighborhood unsupervised and without much support. The Potrero Hill Project area was much more gentrified than the Tenderloin—except for two large public housing complexes plagued by violent crime, which was aggravated by the fact that the curvy layout inadvertently isolated the residents from the rest of the more affluent neighborhood.

"It was harder there," David continued. He hesitated then went on, "The blacks were out to get me. That's when I developed my balance."

I raised my eyebrows. He smiled. "I learned to run on the tops of the fences in those projects because I had to get away fast sometimes."

"Oh." There was a silence, and David looked at me. Finally I said, "Who did you have to talk to?"

"No one."

I waited.

"My dad liked my oldest brother best." Suddenly tears formed in his eyes. He turned his head away.

"Go on."

"Dad told me I was nothing. When he came home at night, all that ever happened was Blam! Hit! Jerk! Slap! It never stopped." For the first time that afternoon, David looked up at me and held my gaze. "Why did he hit me so much?"

A ringing phone interrupted the stillness of the room. I waited for the ringing to stop before saying softly, "I don't know, David. But it's okay to feel sad about it."

His gaze slipped away. "I can't."

"Yes, you can." The fragile moment passed, and I felt him shut down. We needed to keep the conversation moving, so I said, "What did you do then?"

"I had to deal." He shrugged. "I had to, you know, do things."

"Like what?"

His eyes narrowed. "Why are you doing this?"

"Because. What things?"

"Stealing, selling firecrackers, popping meters, you know, stuff."

This young man was enterprising. Then I realized we were missing something. "What about drugs and alcohol?"

"I did get drunk a lot." He paused, "No drugs, except weed. Well, sometimes I took muscle relaxants 'cause I couldn't chill even when I was drunk."

This was serious. Students who had problems with addiction needed a drug and alcohol treatment program, not Summer Search. I remember Lettie calling me to say David had shown up at school drunk one morning. Yet something nagged at me. This boy had few outlets and seemingly almost no adult supervision. The fact that he had almost raised himself, finding the food and other resources he needed on a daily basis, spoke to his strengths under extreme adversity. My therapist side kicked in, and I started speculating. Maybe the price he paid for survival was that he had to bury his feelings. Maybe he couldn't relax because he couldn't unwind, couldn't feel the painful things that had happened to him. Yet they were always there inside him building up steam. What to do? A program popped into my mind. There was a great solution. I had the very program for David: Devil Pups!

Devil Pups was the old-fashioned name for a program for high school boys run by the Marines. Their goal was to teach leadership and good citizenship through a kind of summer boot camp, Marine-style. Macho stuff. David had been emotionally wounded, both by his father and by the threatening neighborhoods where he had somehow managed to cope; masculine validation in a positive context might be just the thing he needed to turn his life in a new direction. When I handed him a brochure describing an experience that most boys would do anything to avoid, his face lit up. "It's perfect," he said, black eyes shining.

In July, David left for his rite of passage—or, in military language, "to get his ass kicked"—in the hot desert of Southern California. He came in first in the cross-country obstacle course and arrived home with several medals from other strenuous events. Running on the top of fences had prepared him well.

Yet, as soon as he came home, he was once again surrounded by the familiar and crushing negativity of his everyday life. Without money, without food, fending for himself, his school attendance began to fall off again. Lettie called to report that David's PO thought a move to another school would solve his attendance problems. "What's a PO?" I asked.

Lettie sighed with exasperation, "Probation officer. Remember? I told you he was on probation for selling firecrackers. The problem is that the school she's recommending is Balboa."

"Balboa," I echoed. "That can't be!" After Wilson had been "reconstituted" in 1993, a misleading word for closed down, Balboa became the high school that served the greatest proportion of minority and disadvantaged students in the city. Only 5 percent of the school population was Caucasian. Known for periods of sporadic violence and low academic achievement, Balboa was a place where David's keen but fragile imagination and intellect would be at even greater risk of remaining underdeveloped. This irrational decision seemed to almost guarantee failure. In fact, on his first day at Balboa, he called to tell me that a Samoan gang attacked him. Although he finally made it into his classroom after only a minor scuffle, he spent the rest of the day worrying about how he was going to get home.

The forces stacked against this boy seemed insurmountable, mocking my efforts to show him something different. I hung up the phone and drove home slowly. When I arrived with a load of groceries, I felt too tired to get out of the car.

Lettie and I both advocated for David to remain at Washington, but we soon learned that once children go into the Juvenile Court system, decisions made by their probation officers are final. So David was transferred from a relatively high performing school in which he had support, friends, and Lettie, to a place where the threat of potential violence dominated all other realities. Feeling helpless, I turned my attention to the other Summer Search students.

The fall wore on. That year, the numbers rose again, and there were now 87 students in the program. They had returned home from their summer experiences, and each one needed to talk and process what they had gone through and what it meant as they returned to the challenges in their lives. The significant shifts and successes they achieved on their trips once again often resulted in friends and even family members backing away. Conversations with someone who understood what they had been through became a lifeline. My evenings were spent returning phone calls. One student, Jose, sobbed as he recounted how his brother had picked him up at the airport returning from his Colorado mountaineering trip. His brother was drunk, and the beat-up pickup truck swerved on the highway. When Jose started to talk about his trip his brother told him to "shut the fuck up." Once home, Jose learned that his parents had separated while he was gone. No one wanted to look at his pictures.

Then there were the financial pressures. After financing so many costly although substantially discounted summer trips, Summer Search needed money. The initial budget had been $30,000. I had since closed my practice and was dependent on Summer Search for a small salary, and office expenses were growing. The budget that year was a staggering $150,000, and I needed to raise an additional $40,000 by year's end. I was beginning to feel desperate, but I knew I couldn't let that show; I had to be confident when speaking to potential donors. The fear, fatigue, and frustration made me disagreeable at home. My beloved husband of 30 years saw the changes in me, and his admiration for the work I was doing became tempered by his frustration at my preoccupation and increasing absences. He told me he wanted me off the phone at night. When I snapped back, "I can't. If I don't keep going, I will never catch up," he left the house for a few hours.

I had to face reality and find a balance. That meant letting go of the small number of students who weren't following through, including David. But then he did something that altered the course of his own life, and mine too.

One morning in the middle of an important conversation with a new donor, I got a collect call from a public phone booth. I took it reluctantly. A familiar voice said, "It's me."

"David?" He was out of breath, and I could hear sirens in the background. "What's going on?"

"It's not my fault; he just kicked us off the bus."

"Where are you?"

"I don't know."

"David, wait, don't hang up. Go home and call me back."

"I can't." His teeth were chattering. "My mother kicked me out of the house last night."

I opened and then closed my mouth. My mind was racing, but I had no idea what to say next. To my relief, he said, "Maybe I'll go see Miss Lupis."

He didn't call back. That evening I phoned his house. I had met his mother and younger sisters at the Summer Search Spring Event; tiny and very thin, all three reminded me of fragile flowers. His two sisters got on the phone now, exclaiming, "David, he can't walk! David falling down!" Then his mother came on the line and said heavily, "David drunk." I had some trouble parsing her thick accent, but finally I understood the words, "Juvenile Hall."

I began to pace. Shouldn't I mind my own business? In an emergency, David had reached out to me, which bound us together. There was no way I could just shrug this off. The next morning, as I drove all the way across the city to Juvenile Hall, I kept questioning the wisdom of my choice. I had absolutely no experience with the juvenile justice system other than the discouraging conversation with David's PO.

Then, unexpectedly, I thought of something that happened when I was in high school. One strange night my mother gathered my sisters and me together and told us that Daddy was in jail. He had gotten into a fight during a card game. She was telling us because it would probably be in the Muncie paper. The next morning he came home with a hangdog expression and a large bandage on his forehead. We never talked about it, but it became yet another burning humiliation at school. I was sure everyone knew about it and was talking about it behind my back.

Juvenile Hall was a large and predictably dismal cement building. After passing through a metal detector, I was told I had to get a pass from David's probation officer. After many wrong turns, I finally found the correct office. The door was half-open, and the officer was laughing on the phone. It sounded like a personal phone call. I waited for almost an hour.

When she finally invited me into her office, I told her I'd come to visit David.

"He's not here."

"Yes, he is."

She waved a list of cases in my face and explained, "You see, he's not on the list."

"I just spoke to his mother."

She got up and stomped down the hall to the main desk. After an animated and lengthy conference with a secretary, she found out that David had used his brother's name. "He's going to pay for this," she grumbled.

We went back to her cluttered office and started over. She asked me, again, who I was and why I was here. I told her, again, about Summer Search, and that David was one of my students. I was tired, I was hungry, and I knew my husband was going to ask me why I was getting in so deep again and why I would be coming home so late—again. Inside, I was screaming, "Just give me a pass, lady!" My smile felt like a grimace. She seemed doubtful as she reluctantly signed a pass, for just one visit.

As we finished, I impulsively reached into my briefcase and handed her the new Summer Search brochure. She took it in both hands, and a photo of a radiant African American youngster participating in a community service program in the Caribbean smiled back at her. A brief flicker of pain crossed her weary face. She tossed it on her littered desk. It slipped off and landed on the floor. I bent down, and picked it up and carefully put it back. Then I lightly touched her shoulder as I passed her chair while walking out the door.

The bleak series of gray corridors were sad and disorienting and the confusion about the name dogged me at each checkpoint. Finally, I came to a locked door with the right number above it. A large African American man welcomed me so kindly. I shook his hand with relief. He smiled and politely pointed out the visitors' area.

When David appeared, his customary cockiness was nowhere to be seen. His eyes were puffy and his hand shook when he waved as he walked toward me. A whiff of his breath alerted the former nurse in me that he was severely dehydrated. He was also extremely pale. The first thing he did was grab me in a full-body hug. He was trembling. When he finally let go, we sat down, and he said, "I didn't do anything."

"Damn it, David, don't give me that bullshit. This is your one and only chance to tell me what happened. Don't blow it."

He launched into a long and convoluted story about getting on a bus while he was high and getting into an argument with the driver. Willie Brown had just been elected mayor, and safety on the municipal buses was his pet project. Not good timing for a swaggering, stoned teenager.

As he was finishing his story, David's tiny, exhausted-looking mother, Lisa, arrived. I watched curiously as she approached him. They stood looking at each other awkwardly. She didn't touch him, and there was a palpable feeling of tension and distrust as they began speaking in rapid Vietnamese. I could only guess, but he seemed to be proclaiming his innocence, while she berated him harshly. She turned to me and said, "David no come home."

I couldn't help but agree. His current unsupervised living conditions were doing him no good and returning to Balboa would only derail any possibility of success.

When I offered to talk with the parole officer and see what we could figure out, Lisa seemed surprised at my concern. Clearly, she was fed up with this son she couldn't control. I didn't blame her.

The man who let me in came up and indicated it was time to leave. I reminded David that I was a former nurse and told him to be sure to drink water and stay hydrated. Then I reached over and gave him another big hug. After we separated, mother and son stood there looking at each other for several long moments. Finally, she reached out with one arm and started to pat him, then tried to hug him. He looked frightened and, even more awkwardly, attempted to hug her back.

This incident helped me understand why so many of the Summer Search students I worked with were so responsive to physical affection. Many of them, like David, came from cultures where parents didn't touch them; others come from homes where physical contact had been violent or had sexual undertones. But even students from more affectionate homes seemed to need this contact as well. Most teachers and other adults in their lives are afraid to hug them for legal reasons, and parents will often refrain from expressing physical affection during the exploding sexuality of the adolescent years. This lack of nurturing can lead teenagers, during one of the neediest and most vulnerable periods in their lives, to seek affection and validation in sexual relationships they are often not mature enough to process emotionally.

Lisa and I made our way out through the dimly lit corridors, but when we finally arrived at the front door, it was locked. Looking through the small glass panel, I could see a desk on the other side, but no one was sitting there. I tried to stifle a feeling of panic, irrationally envisioning a night under lock-down, but then Lisa giggled. We retraced our steps and eventually found another door. As we eagerly slid past the attendant, Lisa turned and put her arms around me. She too needed affection. I hugged her back. She was so small and thin it was like hugging a sparrow. How did this woman find the stamina to work in the restaurant almost 18 hours a day, seven days a week?

At 10:00 AM the next day, I called the parole officer. She was at lunch. I called Lettie. In spite of her counseling caseload, she planned to visit David that afternoon, armed with books she hoped he would crack open out of boredom if nothing else. I told her I was determined to get him out. "But how?" she asked.

"Maybe there's a program of some kind."

The parole officer called late the next day. She was still upset over David's alias and assured me that he was going to stay in Juvenile Hall for quite a while. When he did get out, he would be a ward of the court, and placed in a certified group home. A group home for boys with severe impulse control issues? Is this kid ever going to catch a break? My thoughts were interrupted by the parole officer saying something I couldn't quite catch, something about a knife.

Knife? What knife? I felt sick. I didn't want to hear whatever it was, but I asked her to say it again. It seemed that, when David was high on the bus, he had a knife and had threatened the driver. "I see," I answered slowly. But I didn't see. How could I have gotten Summer Search—and myself—into this?

"This is now a criminal case," the parole officer continued. "I suggest you talk to his lawyer."

When I called his court-appointed attorney to explain that I was looking for a rehab program or to get David into a better environment, he was curious about my interest but unable to provide any suggestions.

I put down the phone carefully. It was almost 5:00 and time to start dinner, but something from a fragment of a conversation was nagging me. Then I remembered. It was with the former director of the San Francisco Conservation Corps, something about how he was planning to start a school somewhere for delinquent but still promising youngsters. What was his name? The next morning, I called the Conservation Corps and was given the name Robert Burkhart. He had indeed started a school in Colorado. Its name was Eagle Rock. Honda had funded it, and the students who were accepted received full scholarships.

My hands shook as I called the school. Miraculously, I was put right through to Robert. After a lengthy discussion, I was convinced that David was exactly the kind of student they were looking for. But the next available date for an interview was in four long months.

Lettie called my office the following day sounding strangely happy as she said, "I have a sister named Loretta in rural Washington State. She lives with her son and his wife; both of them are veterinarians." I waited, biting my lip to keep from interrupting. Finally, she laid it all out: "Loretta has had foster children in the past, and she's willing to take David if Summer Search will pay for his plane fare and other expenses." I was at a loss for words. "David can work on the farm and in the clinic with the animals and go to the local school." The heavy silence between us lengthened. Lettie finally said, "So what do you think?"

"Fantastic, I guess." The complexity of the situation was beginning to feel overwhelming. I looked out the window. There were fresh green leaves on the trees. "Lettie, David had a knife and threatened the driver."

"David would never hurt anyone."

We hung up. I felt that way too, but shadows of doubt made me shudder at the increasing level of responsibility we were all assuming.

I made an appointment with his PO to tell her our plan. She was adamant. "No way. David is a ward of the court, and that's it. Out of state—never."

"Look, he would be with a family that has had foster children and who are willing to assume full responsibility." Seeing her frown, I added, "I just found out that a group home costs the city over $50,000 a year. And I don't think that David needs or would benefit from living with youngsters who need that level of control." I hesitated. Maybe I should have said *treatment*. My eye caught the Summer Search brochure now sitting upright on her desk. I stood up to go. "Can I write up a proposal for the judge at the hearing?"

She looked up at me from behind her sagging desk and offered a slow nod and then smiled.

At the hearing, David, Lettie, and I sat together. Lisa was late, so we saved her a seat. One young person after another was brought before the judge. There were no parents there—or at least no one other than their court-appointed lawyers. The whole scene seemed devoid of optimism and hope. The kids looked so young, so forlorn standing up to face such huge problems alone. Just as it was time to hear David's case, Lisa arrived and slid into place beside us.

The parole officer told the judge that I wished to advocate for David and that I had a highly unorthodox plan. The judge sat quietly, reading the proposal Lettie and I had put together as the entire courtroom sat in silence. Then, without asking a single question, which was unnerving, she agreed to let David go—on the condition that he return and appear before her again in one month's time. A new wave of doubt passed through my mind: another airfare, more money to raise, more explaining to donors. But I let it go. I didn't care. We had won! David was given a second chance.

Lisa, Lettie, and I went directly to the designated area for released inmates. We waited for two hours before David arrived, shuffling along in his soft Juvenile Hall slippers, his shoes and other belongings in a paper sack. He smiled sheepishly as he told us what happened. When he had gone back to tell the wardens about his release, they hadn't believed him, and handed him a mop. Meanwhile, the clerk told us that the boy we were waiting for was not in Juvenile Hall.

When the three of us told David he would be on a plane to Spokane the next day, his face fell. He had been planning on going back to business as usual and was excited about seeing his friends. Lettie and I conferred and decided to give him three days at home if he promised to follow the conditions of his parole: no drugs and home every night by 6:00 PM. We had taken responsibility for him. He gave us his word.

But I didn't trust him. That night I called to make sure David was at home. When he answered, I was relieved. I made a quick decision and asked him to come and speak at a Summer Search board meeting scheduled the next day. He enthusiastically agreed.

David showed up at the meeting on time in yet again another sharp-looking leather jacket. I wondered what was the deal here? As soon as he started speaking, he couldn't stop. "When you grow up in Tenderloin with no mom and no money, you learn how to do things." He flashed his wonderful smile.

As the board heard the details about his entrepreneurial skills and coping mechanisms, I knew they were questioning my decision to stick with this boy. Our mission was to identify future leaders. I understood, but at the same time I felt good about my decision. If I was honest, I couldn't help but feel proud of my rather heroic role in making it all happen. A quiet voice whispered, *Beware—your ego is getting in the way*, but I ignored it.

Very early in the morning, two days later, the phone rang and I heard the now familiar greeting: "It's me."

"David? Wait! You're supposed to be at the airport. Where are you?"

"I wasn't going to see my friends no more, so I wanted to spend the night with them. We fell asleep with the car radio on. When I woke up the battery was dead. I ran down to a telephone booth to call my mom, but she hung up on me."

"David, you lied to me!" Wait a minute, don't push him away now. This was an emergency—not the time to indulge in my feelings. Forcing myself to stay calm, I added, "Call me back in five minutes." I phoned Lisa. She was crying and angry about David's not coming home. I knew how she felt. Speaking calmly and slowly, I managed to convince her to pick him up and take him to the airport. Although he had missed his flight, he would be able to catch the next one in a few hours. With the crisis solved for the moment, I wanted to turn this into a learning experience. How could I get David to engage in introspection rather than blame? He needed to start thinking about why—why did he attempt to sabotage one of the greatest opportunities of his troubled life? But the chance for that discussion wouldn't come until much later.

Despite all the drama, everything seemingly fell into place fairly quickly. David, forever flexible and resilient, began to fit right in with his host family after an uneasy week. "We really like this boy," Loretta told me. "The only problem is he sneaks stuff out of the fridge late at night. It's odd because we've told him to help himself to anything he wants."

After registering at the local school, David got involved in sports. He had always wanted to wrestle. Whenever I called to check on him, he was either at wrestling practice, snowboarding, assisting in surgery for dogs and cats, or making house calls with Loretta's son. It all sounded good, so I just decided to wait about talking to him about sneaking food and hope that he would gradually learn it was okay to ask for what he needed.

He came home to San Francisco for his first monthly report to the judge and then returned to Spokane later the same day. Three months later, after a telephone interview with David, the admissions officer from Eagle Rock called to tell me she thought he was a great fit for their program. They couldn't officially admit him, however, until he came to the school in Colorado for a personal interview and some testing. "Do you by chance have any more students like him?" she asked.

The day before David's trip to Eagle Rock, I was once again interviewing new candidates at Lettie's school. There was a knock on the door. Unusual. I interrupted the interview and walked out into the hallway to see Lettie. Her round face was red and blotched. It looked like she had been crying. "It's David," she said. "He's just been arrested for shoplifting. I don't know what I'm going to do." She started to cry outright as she added, "My family is devastated. Will you call them?"

My mouth was dry, and I felt defeated as I slowly picked up the phone to call Loretta. When she started describing what happened, she let out an involuntary sob. This kind woman had taken a leap of faith; now she felt betrayed—and rightfully so. I struggled to find the right words to console her, but they didn't come. Finally I said, "This isn't your fault, Loretta. There had to be some kind of bump while he was there."

"Yes, but shoplifting! This is a small community. We all know each other."

In spite of the emotion of the moment, I wondered if this might be the chance for David to understand community in a whole different way. Loretta was too upset to hear anything so optimistic. As calmly as I could, I tried to reassure her. "We're in this together," I said, "and we will solve it together. Have David call me at home tonight."

David's voice was maddeningly humble and contrite. To his credit, he told me he had shoplifted many times while there, mostly clothes. Suddenly, I remembered his thing for jackets. All those different and expensive-looking jackets now made sense. It flashed through my mind, this was how he grew up—stealing food to survive, then more expensive things as he grew more nimble and skillful. He was probably addicted to the adrenaline high of shoplifting too. The pattern of surreptitiously sneaking food from the refrigerator even though he had been told he could help himself at any time also made more sense.

"David, just think about this." I paused until I felt I had his full attention. "Tomorrow you are going for your interview at Eagle Rock. It's what you want, right? Then you screw up the day before. Don't you think that's interesting?" He didn't answer, so I continued. "And, you know what? Just before you were to leave for a fresh start with a new family, you did the same thing."

He started to defend himself, but quickly lapsed into silence. I waited a beat. "David, don't shut me out right now. What do you think that stuff means?"

"I don't know. But you're right. It don't make no sense."

An image of my father harvesting soy beans on the columbine—sunrise to sunset, up and down the field, long before the glassed-in cabs—popped into my mind. He would come home with bloodshot eyes and lungs full of dust, then he would blow that hard-earned money on a card game. "No, David, self-defeating behavior does not make sense."

"Linda, I wouldn't do something that don't make no sense on purpose. I think I'm just bad."

Aha, I was on solid ground. "Forget bad. The lazy bum thing won't fly with me, and, besides, that's not it. It's something else. Let's go deeper. Maybe, think about it, just maybe you're afraid of succeeding."

"No." His silence was upsetting. Was he thinking, or had he checked out? Before I could ask a question, I heard a tentative, "Why would anyone be afraid of succeeding?"

"What about your father's voice? Didn't he say you would always be a screw-up?"

"Oh," David said softly. "He also told me I was nothing."

He was quiet. "What are you thinking?" I asked.

"You know, that could be it."

Was this real or was this kid just placating me? No, it seemed genuine. I remembered how fast David could be, how fast he had been from the very start in connecting the dots. I pressed on. "Are you going to screw up your interview tomorrow?" He laughed. With relief I said, "Good. Now listen: Loretta and the family are pretty hurt, so when you get back we need to develop a plan to make things right."

Three days later, Bob called from Eagle Rock School. David had been accepted.

Before leaving the people who had opened their arms and their hearts so generously to him, David did several things. First, he completed a mandatory community service project with the local police department. Then he took the whole family out to dinner with the money he had earned cleaning the vet clinic. At dinner, he read an essay about his time with them, which he had laboriously written and practiced with me on the phone. When he called to tell me about this moment, I closed my eyes to picture this little group having dinner together while experiencing the healing power of gratitude put into words and gratitude shared. After tearfully listening, Loretta helped him understand that stealing from the local store was like stealing from her. For David, this idea was revolutionary.

* * *

By the spring of 1996, a year later, David had charmed the entire staff at Eagle Rock, while also excelling academically. He realized a particular talent in his theater classes and got the lead in *Huck Finn*.

On his short visits home, he managed to keep out of trouble. But there was one last pressing graduation requirement left. "Linda, we have to do something here called a Presentation of Learning for our final senior project. I have to have a suit."

For the next three months, he kept reminding me about this suit he had to have. I realized his obsession went beyond the final presentation: David had adopted a new identity; a suit would be tangible evidence of his significant achievement. Since he had a full scholarship at Eagle Rock, I rationalized that Summer Search could buy a suit for him. Plus, shopping with him would be great fun.

During his next school break, David came to my office for the big event. Too late, it occurred to me I didn't know the best stores to go for men's suits. I called my husband and he suggested J.C. Penney.

The suit selection at J.C. Penney seemed rather old-fashioned, and everything was a bit too large. We needed help, but there were no salespeople in sight. I found a rack of snappy blue blazers. David wrinkled his nose. "I want a white suit."

"I don't think a white suit would be very practical in Colorado, David."

"How about cream-colored with a black shirt?"

As I looked around a little more anxiously for a clerk, a small hunched-over woman in her seventies materialized from behind a large double rack of clothes. She wore heavy costume jewelry, and her feet had what looked like white fuzzy slippers. Her hair was in an old-fashioned beehive and her smile revealed purplish teeth. Immediately it felt like I was right back in Indiana. Only I wasn't. I was with a Vietnamese boy from the Tenderloin who wanted to look like John Travolta in *Saturday Night Fever*!

But even with her help, none of the suits at J.C. Penney could live up to David's fantasy—or fit his slender body. Finally, the saleswoman suggested another department store, which I knew sold significantly more expensive clothes. I began to worry.

We went to Macy's. There were no white suits there either, so we compromised on a light but tasteful turquoise. Of course, we also needed a new shirt, tie, belt, socks, and shoes. By chance, we'd managed to hit a sale, and everything was half off. Still the bill was almost $600, probably more than his family lived on for an entire month. David had just told me that after years of endless toil, his mother had lost the restaurant. It didn't matter; at this moment, he looked so handsome and his pride became mine too.

As he stood, admiring himself in the mirror, I joked, "You better be careful wearing that outfit in your neighborhood. You might get mugged!"

"Damn, I look like a tourist, huh?"

* * *

Several months later, David asked if I could come to the school in Colorado and see him act in *Huck Finn*. "Who needs to come?" I asked him.

"My mother." He laughed. "How come you're always right? Anyway, I need to talk to you. I have to write this paper for English class about how I've changed. You know me best, so what do you think I should say?"

"What do you think?"

"Don't do your question thing, Linda. This time you have to tell me."

"I will, I promise, but tell me what you think first."

"I don't know, it's hard to describe." He paused, and I knew he was thinking. "Can I tell you a story?" Before I could answer, he said, "You know, the last time I went home, my brother, he came in late, like 3:00 in the morning. As usual he was drunk. He was staggering around and he fell down and started sobbing. Everyone swore at him and told him to shut the fuck up." David paused again, "Now I know that's the wrong thing to do," he continued, softly. "I should have gotten up and talked to him or hugged him or something."

I felt my heart flood with warmth. Everything Lettie and I had worked for—all our hopes for this deeply hurt boy—seemed to be coming to fruition. There was no question that David had a manipulative personality. Growing up that had been his strength— that was how he had survived. But now, there was this new ability to empathize, to feel someone else's suffering and to be moved to respond.

David was learning to care about others and feel in a whole new way. Could it be because his suffering had been acknowledged and validated through our long relationship and through the caring circle of people around him?

An impatient voice interrupted my reverie. "I'm waiting, Linda. What do you think?"

I scrambled to gather my thoughts. "Oh. Yes, you are changed, David. There are two important words that might help explain how. Are you up for this?"

"Stop playing games."

"Okay, okay. What I want to talk about is 'empathy' and 'insight.' Do you know what those words mean?"

"You know I don't."

"Empathy, David, means being able to feel what others feel. For the first time, you understood, you actually felt your brother's pain. Right?" He grunted affirmation. "Now that you have this capacity, you will no longer be the prisoner of your own impulses. You can understand and care for others. Next time you will hug your brother even if he swears at you."

My throat was tight with emotion. "David, your life will be different, your life will now have meaning. That caring connection between people: it's everything." I pressed the phone tight against my ear. He seemed to be there with me, but I wasn't sure. I waited.

"What about 'insight'?"

He was with me! "Insight means that instead of blaming other people for your problems, you try to understand the role you play in creating them." A tear began to roll down my cheek. "No longer, David, when things go wrong, will you think you're being picked on. You now have the power to see more deeply, to identify what is within you that can make a situation better or worse. Do you know what I mean?"

"The kids here don't think that way."

"Maybe you can teach them."

"Cool."

We were both suddenly quiet. "Gotta go now," he said and hung up. I put down the phone softly and stood up looking around my living room feeling lost. A few minutes later, the phone rang.

"Linda? It's me. I forgot to say thank you."

* * *

A few months after graduating from Eagle Rock School, David dropped in to see me at the new Summer Search office in San Francisco. My initial happiness quickly faded when I realized he was high. I was aware that he was struggling. After graduation from Eagle Rock he was back home. His first job? A security guard at San Francisco Airport. Yet I was so upset and angry that I kicked him out of the office. Was he never going to stop his self-sabotaging behaviors?

We didn't connect again for a long while, but he was always at the back of my mind. Finally, it was time. I decided to call, leave a message, and see what happened. To my surprise, he called back that same afternoon. He wanted to see me.

At first glance, he looked exactly the same: thin and athletic, bright smile and shining eyes, wearing a tight white T-shirt and baggy jeans. I got in his car, and reached over to hug him. There were tears in his eyes and his whole body was shaking. I was tearful too.

We ducked into a Starbucks. I got my latte and he his mocha and we found a quiet spot. With sudden intensity he asked, "Why did you love me so much?"

I told him I had no idea. As if he hadn't heard my answer, he launched into a monologue that must have been running uninterrupted in his head for a very long time. "You know how I didn't care about nobody. Even my dad..." Here David flushed and changed the subject. "You know when I went to Eagle Rock School in Colorado I learned to care—they taught me to care for the environment. That's what I do now—environmental consulting. You should see all my certificates."

"How is that going, David?"

"Right now? Right now the work is slow, but I have another job next week. I'll be going down to Moss Landing to check out some things on the nuclear plant there. But I started to tell you about my dad. You know, I now have a son, his name is Devin. When Devin met my dad and found out he was my dad he hugged his leg. Just walked right up to him, a stranger, and hugged his leg, just like that! I couldn't believe it.

"So I asked my dad, 'Why did you hit me?' He looked away, but I kept asking him. 'Why did you hit me like that? Why? Dad, it makes me want to hit you now, and that's messed up. So why did you hit me?' He just looked away.

"You know, Linda, you could have been talking to a hardened criminal right now." David smiled, and a hint of his old self, that charm and twinkle, began to show.

It warmed my heart, but also propelled me toward the next question. "What about the drugs?"

"Oh, I don't do that no more."

"Come on, David!"

"Well, I still smoke marijuana sometimes, but that's it. When I turn 30 I think I should just give it up completely." He paused, "You know Eagle Rock School is still going. They want me to come and speak to the kids—I think I will. Maybe I can help them see what it's all about faster. But I have to go now. You still haven't answered me. Why did you love me so much?"

"Stubborn, I guess."

"I didn't care nothing about nobody—I didn't feel anything."

"Yes, but now you do—maybe that's why."

There was a brief silence as we savored this moment together. "I'm a good dad." Then he added, "And I love you, Linda."

"I know. I love you, too."

eight

Unfinished: Myra

The wound of not knowing…that's the one that never heals.

—Adam Johnson

What does it cost to change the direction of an at-risk child? As a society, we are often willing to make substantial investments to help disadvantaged students succeed. Yet most people are unaware of how much money and effort it actually takes to help a student with potential make the complicated transition from the projects to a college campus. And we often become puzzled when those substantial investments aren't enough and even angry when they sometimes backfire, as they so often do and did again and again for a talented young woman named Myra. Myra heard about the private school in wealthy Marin County that gave scholarships from the woman who straightened her hair in Oakland. She won a full scholarship and attended for four years. Tuition in 1994 was about $10,000 annually. Then Myra joined

Summer Search in her sophomore year and participated in two summer trips for a total cost of about $12,000. When she was accepted to Stanford, she was offered $20,000 annually, in combination with a complicated financial aid package that included both Cal and Pell grants, and subsidized loans. Over the course of almost a decade, the cost of the various programs that helped her achieve her educational goals roughly approached almost $200,000. (This was in the early '90s, those costs would be more than doubled today.)

This intelligent and motivated young woman did well at Stanford then mysteriously, just two months before graduation, it all began to fall apart. What happened and why is it that too often so many people pull back at or near the finish line?

Over the years, I've found that one of the most common drivers of an inability to complete important milestones is an underlying negative belief about the self. For youngsters who are unconsciously programmed to perpetuate that negative belief it doesn't seem to matter how much help they have been given or how strong their drive is to succeed. And it's heartbreaking. I began to call this syndrome the "eleventh hour collapse." It was as if—this was an analogy I frequently used with the students—they had been running a marathon, making good time, working incredibly hard, and then, as mile 25 approaches, they begin to lose energy, slow down, sometimes even just stop.

All of us carry within us both negative and positive core beliefs about ourselves from childhood. These beliefs have different names and play out in different ways. Psychoanalyst Joseph Weiss at the San Francisco Psychotherapy Research Group calls the negative messages *pathogenic beliefs*. Children with traumatic or stressful life experiences especially develop pathogenic beliefs about themselves— like "don't trust," "people leave," "I don't matter," "I'm dumb." These negative beliefs often fade from consciousness as they grow, yet they continue to lurk below the surface. If they are not excavated and acknowledged, these unconscious beliefs often act as invisible but powerful roadblocks to creating a fulfilling life. For example, a child who grew up feeling neglected may develop the belief that he *deserves to* be neglected by his parents and others. Or a child who has been told he or she is not worth much will carry a negative belief about succeeding and give up just as they are about to triumph because they believe that their success is somehow not valid or could possibly hurt others.[1]

I know this to be true firsthand. My father's repeated remarks to me and my two sisters— "Don't stand there like dummies"— instilled in us the belief that not only were we dumb but we were also incapable of learning. This belief became more unconsciously pressing even as—or especially when—we achieved beyond what any of us expected. We were still damaged goods, and damaged goods are not supposed to become successful. As a result, success in our twenties and thirties brought with it, for all three of us, a certain vague discomfort that manifested most frequently as a tendency to lose energy just before we completed something important.

In the early years of my marriage, I was convinced my brilliant husband didn't think I was smart or competent. Of course, I helped perpetuate that belief by often "forgetting" to follow through and complete tasks that were important to him. That behavior triggered criticism that I both dreaded and at the same time expected—maybe even unconsciously counted on. There is comfort in the familiar, an odd sense that it is "right," even when in reality it's painful and dead wrong. Doing the hard, inner work of bringing those childhood beliefs to light, seeing them for what they were, and eventually letting

---

1. Weiss, Joseph. "Control-Mastery Theory," In *Encyclopedia of Psychotherapy Volume* 1 (2002), San Francisco Psychotherapy Research Group, San Francisco Psychoanalytic Institute and University of California.

them go, helped me understand how to intervene as I watched so many Summer Search students lose energy just as they approached the success for which they had worked for so long and so hard.

For many low-income hard-working students, the "eleventh hour collapse" happens most frequently during their senior year of high school. Often the first in their family to qualify for college, on the brink of stepping into new and wonderful opportunities, these students began to lose focus, screw up their financial aid packages, forget deadlines, stop returning my calls, and sometimes just disappear. Success, the great unknown, is just too alien and therefore terrifying—much more terrifying than the familiar default: failure. Success challenges the unconscious messages so many these students share: *I am destined for failure. I don't deserve this. I don't belong in college.*

No student struggled with the issue of completion more than Myra, a highly competent young woman who had both internal grit and external opportunity. As a stellar student since kindergarten, she had an abundance of affirmation from her home, school, and church but it came with a price: weirdness with her less academically able sibling, loss of friendships from peers who in grade school were already slipping in school and in life, and being the only successful black student at her private high school. For Myra, as her successes mounted, achievement came to represent loneliness and alienation.

Myra's private high school didn't serve the usual Summer Search demographic. It was a school with extensive resources located in Marin, one of the wealthiest counties in the United States. Like most private schools this school was interested in diversity and provided full scholarships to promising minority students. Myra commuted to school from West Oakland, which was an hour or more away, depending on traffic. On one bright morning in 1993, I set off to interview six of these students. I was curious what it would be like.

When Myra walked into the small private room in the library the first thing I noticed was her energy. She beamed a huge smile, and laughed when she shook my hand. At about 5'2" with almond skin and dark eyes, she was petite and extremely attractive. She soon seemed to be larger than life as her outgoing personality began to fill the room. I remembered reading that one aspect of resilient children was they were often described as "cuddly" babies, an advantageous attribute to cultivate when attention is a limited commodity.[2] Myra's infectious warmth certainly made her a cuddly teenager. She was easy to like. Of course, she knew that I was offering scholarships of some kind and so had turned on the charm. It was clear that she fully intended to qualify for Summer Search, whatever that meant.

I looked at Myra's transcript and saw that she was high-performing. Her poise and sophistication, as well as her good grades at this rigorous school, made me question: did she really need the additional help that Summer Search offered? I went back and forth whether to accept her into the program. At that moment, who could have ever known that just sixteen years later, this young woman would sing at my husband's funeral.

I did wonder how Myra made the daily two-to-three-hour, round-trip journey from her home in West Oakland to school on public transportation—surely a disorienting experience for anyone. Not only from West Oakland but she lived in the Acorn Projects, an area with a troubled history that went back to the late '50s. At that time due to the high level of violence the Oakland Redevelopment Agency decided to clean them up and demolished almost every pre-existing structure, dislocating over 9,000 residents. Although new apartments were constructed, the sense of community was lost.

---

2. Werner, Emmy E., and Ruth S Smith, *Vulnerable, but Invincible: A Longitudinal Study of Resilient Children and Youth.* McGraw-Hill, 1982.

Efforts to bring that spirit back failed along with efforts to bring in economic and racial diversity. Today, those failures have resulted in an enormous housing project that's known for drugs and violence populated almost entirely by low-income African Americans. The Acorn Projects are also infamous as the place where Huey Newton, founder of the Black Panther Party, was murdered in 1989.

In the interview, we were—literally and figuratively—miles away from her life in those projects as we sat around a beautiful wooden table with leather chairs. Instead of the kind of tiny stifling spaces with stale air where I usually interviewed students, at the end of this small room were tall stately rectangular windows looking over opulent grounds with rolling green grass and trees. When I asked Myra how it felt to daily navigate between two such different cultures and communities she shrugged and said she felt lucky. She loved school and her various roles in the choir and student government. She also felt grateful because she had the chance to develop talents that elsewhere would have been neglected.

I wanted and asked for more. Myra sat up straight and looked at me intently for a few seconds, her wide smile vanishing. "I know you want me to tell you what my life in West Oakland is like, how hard it is—but I'm not going to do that." She waved her hand around the room and continued. "Appearances in this place are so important. It takes all my energy to keep up a façade and pretend that my life is normal. That's the only way I can handle having to live a double life. Please don't take that away from me."

I paused and looked at Myra more closely. For the time being, I was just going to have to accept what she could offer. She had only mentioned her parents in passing—she lived alone with her mother, and her father was not much in her life. Obviously, her life was more complicated than her positive, careful presentation let on. I tried one last time. "I hear you, but can you just give me just one paragraph about what it's like for you at home?"

Myra paused and spoke with a slight edge. "Okay. My mother works really hard taking care of some sick lady in San Francisco. She's gone all week. I come home alone every night and it's late. By the time I get home I can't go outside because of the gunshots so I study for a few hours, eat some cold cereal, and go to bed as early as I can so I can get up at 5:30 to start the next day. I do this every day."

"Thank you. I appreciate that picture, which confirms what I have already guessed."

"What's that?"

"That you're incredibly motivated and incredibly brave." Myra's lower lip trembled just a bit and she waved a hand over her face.

Time to move on. I decided to throw her a curveball. "How about slowing down and getting in tune with yourself in a whole different way?"

"Okay. What exactly do you have in mind?"

"A wilderness expedition in Colorado with Outward Bound. For a month."

Myra looked confused. I bet she was thinking "Why on earth would I want to do something like that?"—but she just smiled and nodded. It was a strange suggestion, but she was used to taking advantage of opportunities, and she was motivated. Her eyes widened and she laughed as she accepted this crazy-sounding offer without really thinking it through.

Over the next few months, Myra checked in regularly to report on the fitness training she was doing, as required both by Outward Bound and by Summer Search. Then, just one month before she was due to leave, she stopped calling. When I finally reached her, she said she had decided not to go. Never before had a student cancelled so late or so casually.

As Myra began to glowingly describe a gospel music conference in Atlanta—her dream trip—I tried to not interrupt. "This is something I have always wanted to do and the dates conflict with the wilderness program. I will find the $400 somehow."

I started to say something critical about her not following through, but a small voice warned me not to react. I didn't know why. Then the image of her sitting by herself eating cold cereal every night came to mind. So alone was this girl.

Later, I realized she had never said she was sorry. Shouldn't I have confronted her more pointedly? Maybe another time. For now, she was more vulnerable than she appeared and my support and acceptance was probably essential in helping her manage the high-wire balancing act that was her current life. Although I was annoyed by her casual rejection of the opportunity I'd given her, at the same time I found myself admiring her determination to pull herself forward. I decided to call her back. When I told her that Summer Search would pay her airfare along with the modest tuition, there was a shocked silence. Then she offered what felt like a perfunctory thank you. Feeling slightly unsettled, I said good-bye. Before long, school was out for the summer and she was on her way to Atlanta.

After her trip, Myra sent in the required essay describing the joys of living and performing with some of the best gospel singers in the U.S. When she talked about deciding not to go on the Outward Bound trip, she wrote: "When I told Mrs. Mornell I didn't want to go on a wilderness expedition, I expected that almost middle-aged white woman to throw me out of the program."

Almost middle-aged! What a charming description of me! I had just turned 52 and couldn't help chuckling. But the remark was revealing. Maybe she had "hoped" I would throw her out of the program. Why? What underlying negative messages about herself was she harboring? Why was she so guarded? I still didn't know who this girl really was. But she was in the program, and two summer trips were becoming the norm for every student. That meant it was time to plan for the next step.

Given the many demands on her time, Myra didn't call in as regularly as most of the other students, so we didn't talk all that much during the school year. In January when we met for the second interview to decide about another summer program I asked her, "How do you think it would feel to live in an academic environment without the three-hour commute?" What I didn't ask her was how it would feel to be on a more equal footing with her peer group.

Myra's eyes lit up. "You mean how would it feel not to worry if I'll have enough money every day for the bus? How would it feel to live in a dorm? Oh Linda, I would love to do that."

I gave her a brochure describing Choate Rosemary Hall, the same program several Summer Search students had taken to travel to France, only this opportunity was strictly academic and run on their boarding school campus in Connecticut. For the first time, Myra could experience academic life without having to ration her daily energy. She could work hard in the mornings and then relax and have fun in the afternoons, as her schoolmates did without thinking.

When she came home, we met at her school. I jumped right in. "So tell me, what was it like?"

Myra closed her eyes and smiled. "Grass. There was grass everywhere." She paused and hummed for a moment before continuing rapidly. "The way the campus works is that there are these buildings, sort of like a crescent shape with grass in between. During the day after classes there are soccer games going on, sometimes twelve games at once. I am a terrible soccer player but I loved playing on that grass. There were times I remember being in awe. I would just start running back and forth creating wind on soft grass that moved under my feet."

This image brought tears to my eyes but Myra was moving on. "Socially it was good. There were even black people there! They were called the Connecticut scholars—black kids from poor areas who were smart. It was a great summer." Myra paused and smiled again. "I had my first kiss. He was a guy from Nigeria. He was half white but he claimed Nigerian. His dad was rich."

I couldn't help smiling then Myra's tone changed. "What I regret about my summer is that I tended to hang out with the kids I was comfortable with—meaning the black kids." She continued, "I just couldn't help it. It's so hard—there are so few of us at my school."

I asked the inevitable question: how had she changed? She paused again. "Now that I'm home I know it changed me but I can't quite articulate why. One thing though. It felt so strange to feel safe… always safe, even at night. My life in West Oakland is so hard. Public transportation every day to school is so hard. Everything is dangerous but at the same time it's normal. I always worry about being gang raped and left in the park. People are dying around me but I worry about rape. I wear loose clothes, big sweatshirts and baseball caps—anything to hide my body and face—and then put them in my backpack once I get to school. But at Choate," Myra smiled, and as she continued there was a dreamy expression on her face. "Week after week, I felt safe. I guess it was like feeling…*care free*. Now that I am home I miss that feeling so much."

* * *

In January, Myra arranged for a group of gospel singers from her church to perform at her school—a big first for both communities. Although I rarely had the time to go to athletic competitions, plays, or graduations, I decided I had to attend this one—and I was glad I did. The stately auditorium at Branson rocked that night, big time.

Myra's voice was especially powerful as it rose above the chorus. She introduced her choir members one by one with obvious pride.

Afterwards, she was surrounded by friends, so I slipped out. Just as I was leaving, the crowd parted and I got a full view of her from the back. The heels of her shoes were broken down and there were holes in her stockings. My heart clenched; what else was hidden behind the competent and polished façade this young woman so skillfully presented to the world? What parts of herself did she have to suppress to remain so positive? What underlying and unknown wounds did she carry?

Then, that spring, a student from the projects of West Oakland received an acceptance letter to Stanford University. Talented, beautiful, and smart, Myra had hit an exceptionally high benchmark of what the world defined as success. She was the pride of her school and community, as well as a great poster child for Summer Search. Her inauspicious origins and the grueling daily realities of her previous life faded even further from view as she donned the elite mantle of a Stanford undergraduate.

During her college years, Myra graced and sang at a number of Summer Search events. Her musical talents, her huge voice, and outgoing personality were always a hit. An extravert, she was interested in everyone and mixed easily with the crowd. Then, in her senior year, she stopped returning my calls. I felt a creeping fear. Was the eleventh hour collapse a possibility for this highly motivated young woman? Surely not.

One evening that spring Myra resurfaced, her familiar voice apologetic and embarrassed. She was living off-campus and getting ready to graduate. A sudden and uncharacteristically emotional rush of feelings and words revealed the real reason for her call. She was in a terrible bind and couldn't pay her half of the rent. There were only two months to go before graduation, and she had no one to go to. Could Summer Search help?

John Osterweis, our founding board chair, had urged me from the very beginning to develop a special fund for alumni who needed emergency aid in college. At first, I'd resisted because I was overwhelmed with the needs of the high school kids. However, as our early Summer Searchers went off to college, it became clear that even with generous financial aid packages, so many of them needed some kind of safety net. John was right. It's hard enough for any young person to successfully launch into adult life. To do so without the backing of supportive adults who are able to help smooth over the inevitable speed bumps of college life is even harder.

The Bernard Osher Foundation stepped in with a generous annual grant for emergency aid and enrichment funding so Summer Search could support our students in college. Just knowing that someone had their backs was a psychological saving grace for many of the kids—even if they never ended up asking for help. In Myra's case, after all her hard work, it was unthinkable that she not graduate. It was also unnerving to realize the significant resources that had been invested in her for so many years could all be rendered pointless by eight hundred dollars, two months' missed rent. I told her that, of course, Summer Search could help with her emergency. Relief flowed over the phone line. For now we could relax.

In July, I made a routine call to Stanford to verify Myra's graduation data as part of documenting our alumni statistics. Myra had finished the school year six units short of the requirements. She did not graduate.

Why had she pulled back, just short of the finish line? And dammit, why hadn't she called me? Those questions pounded in my head. I wasn't sure how to reach her and I wasn't sure I even wanted to speak to her—I was afraid of what I might hear and in truth what I might say. I was still running Summer Search alone, so once again I allowed the enormous needs of the other students to distract me.

A few months later Myra called; she was her usual upbeat, cheerful, and chatty self. I listened warily as she gave an update on what was happening in her life, which included references to her recent "graduation." She told me she had been living at home with her mom for a while, but she had recently gotten her own apartment in Oakland and had a great job with Sony. Abruptly, my heart pounding, I interrupted her.

"Myra, what happened?"

"What do you mean?"

"I called the school. What happened?"

"It's hard to explain."

The silence grew heavy. With a note of warning in her voice Myra said, "Linda, my self-worth depends on forgetting everything that happened before that day I never graduated."

"Yeah, but guess what? That way of dealing with it may work for a while, but it's based on a lie." There was no response, so I said again, "Tell me what happened."

"I don't want to."

If only all of us could understand that so often what adolescents and young adults need and want is the exact opposite of what they say they do. I waited for a long minute. Then I said, "I know. Tell me anyway."

It came in a rush. "The summer after my junior year, I had an internship with Sony in New York. I did my financial aid online before I left." She hesitated, "When I got back to school, I thought the money part was all worked out, and I started classes. Everything was okay. Then the second semester I began getting letters, somehow my aid applications were all messed up. I was also short on my rent.

You and Summer Search fixed that so I thought the rest would work out too. I tried to straighten it out, but nothing worked. There wasn't enough money. I didn't know how to fix it, so I just…" Myra let out a long sigh. "I tried to ignore that it was happening. I didn't tell anyone about it and kept going to classes and pretending I was like everyone else, even though the school told me I was no longer a registered student since my tuition wasn't being paid."

"It's hard to imagine living with that kind of denial."

Myra continued, with increasing urgency. "The night before graduation, there was a special ceremony for the black students. I went, but inside I was screaming, 'I'm not one of you. I didn't make it.' But there were the grandmothers, the aunts and daughters and brothers and everyone else, it seemed impossible to do anything but to keep on faking it."

There was a sudden halt to this honest conversation. Something was wrong. I asked Myra what she was thinking, but she didn't respond. I waited.

"Linda, I don't want to play your silence game anymore. I gotta go."

"Wait, you have to help me out here."

"You wanted me to graduate from Stanford. That's all you cared about just like everyone else."

"Whoa! Myra, hold on. That's what *you* wanted, what we both have worked towards for so long."

"Yeah, well, there is a lot you don't know."

"I think that has been true from the very beginning."

Myra's voice wavered. "When I finally graduated high school and look back now, I realize the cost of those terrible commutes, the pressure of everybody being so rich and having such easy lives and how I pretended to belong. The same thing happened at Stanford.

My mother wanted me to come home but I almost never did. I cut myself off from everyone and felt even more alone than I did in high school." Myra stopped for a minute, and then continued, "It's strange, but now I mostly feel just…really tired."

"No wonder.… "

Myra interrupted me. "No, listen. I'm worn out. I just want to rest, and sleep. I feel like I've been in a battle, for years, and I guess I know I have what it takes to win. Only I can't remember what I was fighting for."

I longed to help us both make sense of what she was saying, make it come together, find some way of defining what should come next. Before I could think how, Myra abruptly switched gears. "People out here in West Oakland are talking about me running for the school board. What do you think?"

Without thinking, I reflexively answered. "That's crazy. You need to invest in yourself right now before doing anything to help others."

She laughed. "I knew that's what you would say. Thanks, Linda."

After that Myra told me she would call her advisor at Stanford to find out what she needed to do to complete those final six units. Before we got off the phone, I could hear the relief and gratitude in her voice. She promised that whatever happened, she would keep talking to me and not go underground with her feelings again.

* * *

I reminisced about Myra's first interview—how I had almost passed on her because I thought she would be okay without Summer Search. It was an important lesson, relearned. No matter how resilient the child, or how many resources at his or her disposal, it's extremely difficult to overcome the dysfunctional behaviors and negative beliefs triggered by poverty. I recalled a conversation we had during her sophomore year at Stanford. She was living on campus near the fire station. As she called in to report on how it was going, she said, "You know, Linda, the other night the fire alarms went off and the sound of those sirens almost made me feel homesick."

Yet it all came to nothing. Two months later, Myra called and left a short message. She had a good job offer and relocated to Atlanta. The phone calls continued infrequently, all of them ending the same way: with my insisting she complete those six units, and her insisting it didn't matter. I didn't hesitate to point out that listing Stanford on her resume made her efforts to build a solid, truthful life for herself a sham. I also tried to talk to her about possible old negative beliefs that might be holding her back. But my ideas and words weren't being heard. This was something she would have to discover on her own. Maybe the cost of functioning at such a high level while pretending everything was okay made insight hard to come by. Or maybe there was something else I didn't understand.

Finally, eight years after her faux graduation, Anndretta called to tell me she had returned to Stanford! She was finishing her Bachelor of Arts while also getting a Masters in Interdisciplinary Humanities. I was quietly—cautiously—thrilled. I wondered what would happen next. And I waited.

Just two months before this graduation, without consulting me, Myra sent another request to the Summer Search alumni emergency and enrichment fund. Her funding had fallen through. This time she needed $5,000 immediately or she would not be able to graduate. With mixed feelings, I explained to the staff person who oversaw the fund that we should approve the request with the understanding that she call me immediately.

It took three weeks. When Myra did finally call, she was nervous. "Linda, thank you for believing in me. I'm so grateful."

"Oh? The decision I made had nothing to do with believing in you—in fact, I am incredibly resentful. I feel blackmailed into supporting, or, you might say, rescuing you once again. It is okay to apply to the Bernard Osher Fund—that's what it's for—emergency aid. But do you think it was okay to do it so impulsively and without talking to me?"

"It's just that they told me I had the funding and then it fell through at the last minute."

"Please, don't even go there."

There was an audible groan. "You're right."

"There's only one way I can be right and that's for you to complete what you need to do. Finish. Let go of whatever is holding you back and be the person you have worked so hard to become. Do you hear me?"

One month later, just before graduation, a letter arrived:

Dear Linda,

I really don't know how to put this into written words. A song would be more effective in communicating how I feel—but for now this letter will have to do. I am grateful. Extremely thankful that you gave me the support when I could not figure out any other way to pay Stanford. But it's more than that now. More than happy-to-get-bailed-out. Again. My gratitude is not just for this particular occurrence of kindness. The thing that really gets me is the fact that it's been such a long journey over such a long time. I've taken so many detours. So many steps sideways and even backwards and it has taken so long to figure out why. My appreciation is not just about the money—I am overwhelmed with gratitude for all the time and attention you have given me since I was fifteen years old. No matter what I do, I just can't seem to wear you out. Really. I think on some level I have been trying to ditch you and for whatever reason, you just won't retreat. I am very affected by that truth. Resilient? That's you actually. That resiliency means so very much to me. That is what I aspire to be. Not a resilient victim, but a resilient Giver. On March

15th I will have finished my undergrad work completely. My next hurdle is to finish the requirements for the co-terminal MA program so that I can graduate June 15th with both degrees. Be on the lookout for that cream-colored envelope. Big Hug! Myra

* * *

What can be learned from this fifteen-year investment—by Summer Search and so many other institutions—in a single student? I think the lesson we all need to realize is that with change, with opportunity, *there is always loss.* Today, with new Summer Search students, I teach staff to talk to kids from the start about how achieving, how rising above will feel—for so many it will be an experience they have never known. Start the dialogue about how it will feel to become different from their peers and family, to stand alone—at least in the early years.

The graduation was not only a healing experience for Myra but for her whole family. When she received her degree, she was surrounded by them all, and her father hooded her. She sang.

Myra went on to win a full fellowship at UCLA where she was accepted into a PhD program in critical performance studies. She will graduate in the spring of 2015 with a doctoral degree in theatre and performance and plans to become a college professor, published scholar, and a role model for her community. She continues to work hard to become her most authentic self and she has married a wonderful man.

When I think about this young woman today, an image comes to mind. During Myra's junior year at Stanford, one of our board members, Sally Hambrecht, asked her to perform at a political fund-raiser in her home in San Francisco. Myra, on her way toward becoming a resilient Giver, ended up singing for one of the most resilient and ultimately successful youngsters of all time: Bill Clinton.

nine

Discounted and Discarded: Levar

There came a time when the risk to remain tight in a bud was more painful than the risk it took to blossom.

—Anaïs Nin

The concept of foster care is ancient. There have always been parents who are unable to care for their children, and so it makes sense to create a structure that provides homes for those children, homes where they're supposed to be cared for by functioning adults who have the time and energy to add a child to their household. Still, foster children are sometimes called "orphans of the living"[1] because they've been abandoned in a profoundly fundamental way, by parents to whom they are still connected by a powerful biological bond.

As of this writing, there are almost half a million youth in foster care in the U.S. Teenagers represents the largest group of these and the

---

1. Toth, Jennifer. *Orphans of the Living: Stories of America's Children in Foster Care.* New York, N.Y. Simon and Shuster. 1997.

statistics as to how well they do are fairly grim. Academically, foster care children perform well below capacity. Fewer than 45 percent will graduate from high school. A year later after they age out of the system at 19, 30 percent of the boys will have been incarcerated and the girls will be two and a half times more likely to become pregnant than their nonfostered peers. Within four to six years of their "emancipation," 51 percent will be unemployed and a third will have acquired serious mental health problems. Some data suggests 30 percent of the homeless population in this country were in foster care as children.[2] Just as Solaria taught me the realities of what it meant to be ambitious and talented and undocumented, a student named Levar taught me about the harsh realities and long-term impact of being placed in foster care at the age of seven. Breaking out of the deep insecurities that this placed on his psyche and his soul would be a long battle for us both.

2. Beam, Chris, *To the End of June: The Intimate Life of American Foster Care*. New York: Houghton Mifflin Harcourt, 2013, 101–102.

Levar stumbled into the counseling room at Oakland High to get his initial interview. A gangly sophomore at the time with an essay in hand, he had the look of a child who had not been cared for. His skin had a greasy sheen, and there was food in his teeth. His clothes were clean but the lines on his once-checkered shirt were almost indistinct from many washings. In spite of his appearance and the smeared handwriting and crumpled paper of his initial essay, there was a hint of real potential. His description of his leadership abilities: "I was always a leader in my school. I was the first one to break a window and the first to get into a fight." On describing his problems with concentration, he wrote: "When a pencil dropped, I was on it."

The referring teacher at Oakland High, Georganne Ferrier, was a graduate from that school, which historically served middle-class as well as low-income students. But by 1994 the population was a combination of low-income African American and Latino kids who mixed uneasily with the large influx of desperately poor immigrants from Vietnam, Laos, and Cambodia. Severely overcrowded, the atmosphere was tense.

Just as Levar and I started to talk, a school counselor abruptly opened the door without knocking and sat down at the other end of the table. She then pulled out her lunch and started eating. "Didn't you see the sign on the door? This room is reserved for Summer Search interviews all day," I said. The woman looked up angrily and continued eating. "As you can see, obviously, Levar and I are engaged in a private interview," I pressed.

"This is a counseling room," she responded. "And it's my school." Heat rushed to my face. Why was she so angry? Levar put his hand on my arm and said, "Calm down. Let's go get Mrs. Ferrier."

Wait a minute. Who was in charge here? Apparently, it was Levar, who was already heading out to look for her room. I suppressed my irritation and amusement at the incongruity of the situation, and meekly followed him through a large hallway jam-packed with the noise and energy of too many kids throbbing with too much energy crammed into too small a space.

The door of Mrs. Ferrier's room was locked, and the small window was covered with paper. Levar knocked again more forcefully. We were walking away when the door opened ever so slightly. A small, harried-looking woman whose glasses were perched on her nose at an angle peered out cautiously. When we told her what had happened, she whispered that she couldn't leave her room. We needed to go back to the counseling office. She would call ahead.

After a prolonged negotiation with two indifferent administrators, Levar and I finally relocated to a tiny airless room the size of a large closet and began again.

Georganne Ferrier, the only public high school teacher to respond to my initial letter describing the program in 1990, was by 1994 Summer Search's longest referring partner. As a result, the students at Oakland High knew what to do in the interview. It was their chance to tell their story, and they knew to grab that opportunity. In fact, I joked with her that I seldom got the chance to ask the "shoes" question.

Like the students before him, Levar began talking immediately and frankly about his childhood. Years later, he would describe that interview in a speech:

> I was raised by the foster care system, where I learned to build a wall around me to protect myself from the outside world and my own feelings. Because I was constantly moving, I never got to keep anything as my own. I wanted to be dead to the reality that I never had a father and that my mother used drugs and that I would become another lost soul. In my interview with Linda, I opened up my deep scars and wounds to her because she seemed to care and did not condemn me, as so many had before.

Almost immediately I knew this young man was a candidate. In spite of his unkempt presence and troubled history, Levar had a directness about him, an unusual ability to talk specifically—almost poetically—about himself, almost as though he were on the outside looking in. I was determined to find a place for him with Summer Search. But he was full of expansive, if unrealistic, zeal about what opportunities the program might offer.

> I told her that I had trouble concentrating and that I wanted to go to Africa. Linda said I was too immature to go to Africa, but she had a plan to help me with my concentration.

With very little effort I was able to convince Levar to take a trip so difficult that it had a hard time attracting both affluent and scholarship students alike. Given his history of instability, I figured that the longer the experience the better. My recommendation was based on three factors: 1) it was practical—the program had one of the last openings available; 2) it was psychologically appropriate—seven long weeks would give Levar the chance to fully immerse himself in a new and challenging environment; and 3) it was familiar—run by Chewonki in Maine, one of my favorite institutions. The trip, an extremely strenuous program, was poetically named the "Thoreau Wilderness Expedition"—although a more accurate title might be "Do or Die."

Levar didn't question this recommendation. In fact, he enthusiastically agreed to go on what I described to him as a very difficult and quite long hiking and canoeing expedition in the wilds of northern Maine.

> I walked through mud with an 80-pound canoe on my shoulders. The next thing I know is my shoe falls off, but I keep going with just one shoe. That was the beginning of the end of my lack of concentration.

When Levar returned home, his ability to concentrate had, indeed, greatly improved. He wrote an excellent follow-up essay and called in once or twice. Then, silence. As the annual Fall Event at Oakland High School approached, I counted on him coming and called several times to remind him, but there was no response. That night to my great disappointment, there was no sign of him. When Mrs. Ferrier called the next day she told me that he had come, but very late. I was somewhat reassured—but I wondered what had happened.

> The inner city is a place, but the ghetto is a state of mind. I returned, full of life and vigor, only to face the same negative mind-state I felt would never change. The wall I built to hide from the world began to choke me.

What had actually happened to this boy? Why, after such a big success, did he pull back? I called after the event to tell him how disappointed I was and how important he was to me and to the program. Then I stressed the importance of celebrating what had been one of his greatest successes to date. That meant showing up. After some hesitation, he began to talk more about how he had grown up. As I listened, it slowly dawned on me that sticking with anything was completely alien to him.

"Linda, I don't like to talk about what happened because of the judgment. It's important that you know my mom was a good mom. She took care of us three boys and had a steady job before things fell apart. My dad, well, he didn't stick around. I didn't see him until I was 13. Anyway, we lived in the Acorn Projects in West Oakland. Do you know about them?

"Yes," I said, thinking of Myra. "I know about them, for sure. Really hard, huh?"

Levar didn't answer; he just kept telling his story. "At that time the crack cocaine epidemic hit the projects hard. My mom stayed clean but lost her job. One way people in the projects make money is to let the dealers pay them to use their apartment. That's what she did to pull us through. There were strange people in and out all the time. I didn't know it, but they were dealers.

"Then my mom couldn't hold on anymore, and we lost our apartment. That's when she started using, too." There was a long pause. "We lived in other people's houses and sometimes on the streets. Until that day I will never forget."

Levar stopped, and I wasn't sure what to do. This had to be hard. "It was the day before my oldest brother's birthday," he continued. "August 15, 1986, the day we were put into foster care. What happened was crazy. We were real hungry, always hungry, and that day we were ready to go to St. Vincent de Paul in Oakland to stand in line to get food. My older brother showed up late, so we missed lunch. My mother grabbed him and whipped him in public. Someone called the police, and they took us all to jail. My mom was crying, saying she was so sorry."

"I am hearing you, Levar."

"So at seven," he continued, "I went into foster care. For the next two years I lived in seven foster homes. I remember the first one—those people were white. I kept peeing the bed, peeing everywhere I was so scared. Then moving around so much you sort of get used to being discarded and stop even wondering what will happen next. Coming home from school, you never knew if a social worker would be there waiting with all your clothes in a sack on the porch."

His tone changed. "How did you expect me to trust Summer Search? It scared me that you were waiting for me at the Fall Event. I can't count on anyone, and I had started to count on you."

"Okay. I get it now."

"Finally, I was taken in," he paused, "by the Reverend James Windom and his wife, Lucille. They kept me until I was 16. The reverend never introduced me as his foster child. He either called me boy or son. He even broke the law by not reporting my fights at school or my bedwetting. You're not supposed to punish foster children, and when I misbehaved he broke the law again and got out the belt. That's how he treated his own son."

"My mom came every week. Her last visit was sometime in '89. She was in real bad shape, so skinny and shaky. The following Saturday I waited for her as usual, but she didn't show. I remember sitting on that couch in the living room and starting to cry. It was covered in plastic. I can still hear the sound of my tears dropping on that plastic coating."

After that conversation, Levar disappeared again and didn't return my calls. Then the telephone was disconnected. I was left to wonder if I would ever see him again. Finally, in January of 1995, four long months later, he called to check in. His foster mother, Lucille, had died, so his foster father had moved to Sacramento to be closer to his grandchildren, taking Levar with him.

Just as I was trying to digest this information, Levar asked, "When are you coming for my next interview?"

His next interview? Sacramento was a three-hour drive from my office, and besides, Summer Search was supposed to serve Bay Area students. There were limits, I told myself early on a clear March morning, as I got into the car to make the long trip north.

Right away, I saw Levar was in trouble. I looked at him with concern. He stared back, but there was a scary blankness in his eyes. When he talked, his speech was slowed, almost slurred. He looked even more unkempt. His clothes were rumpled, and there was mucus in his eyelashes and food again in his teeth. His new school was much more challenging academically, and he was struggling. Then there was the move. There had been so many moves. He didn't have the energy to make friends again.

Looking at him now, I wondered if the childhood deprivation that so weighed him down was going to break him. That's when he told me he still wanted to go to Africa.

"Levar, I think you need to do something academic this summer."

"More school? I can't hack it right now."

"That makes sense," I agreed. "No point in going to school if you can't focus." I paused to think. "You take Spanish, right?" He smiled faintly, pleased that I had remembered. "What about a family home stay in a Spanish-speaking country? It might be helpful to learn to speak and to think in another language. Good for the concentration, you know."

> I found my love for family, ambitions for a future, and a chance to see who I really was in a place called Spain. My new family saw me as a gifted, caring, strong, and funny young man, who had simply received a terrible start in life. Soon I began to see myself in the same light as they did.

After Levar returned from Spain, he left his foster family—the Reverend had remarried—in Sacramento and returned to Oakland to live with his mother, who was still struggling with drug addiction. I was perplexed by the decision. Why would a boy forcibly removed from his biological family and in foster care for eight years so abruptly be allowed to return to the same situation?

Levar, now ready to start his senior year of high school, wanted to return to Oakland High to graduate. As a foster kid heading toward high school graduation and emancipation, he was about to run out of options. I later learned that this often triggers a return to the birth parent, a fact that the foster care system denies.[3]

---

3. Beam, *To the End of June*, 179.

When he called in the fall of 1996, he reported he was doing better. It was good to be back in Oakland and with Mrs. Ferrier. Then his communications again became infrequent, and I lost track of him for several months. In the winter of 1997, I was interviewing new as well as ongoing students at Oakland High School. Levar didn't show up for his appointment.

To my relief, he arrived at the very end of the day. His energy was low but the deep and scary sadness I had seen the year before in Sacramento was gone. He also looked much better physically. He had applied to colleges: NYU, Morehouse, and Berkeley. I was heartened by his aspirations but wondered if those schools were too ambitious, given his ongoing struggles with depression and his spotty academic performance in the all-important junior year. The young man who had so successfully navigated the inept adults around him in our first hour together, now smiled indulgently. He had already been accepted to his first choice: Morehouse! But, he added with a deep sigh, he didn't feel ready. He also didn't have the money, so, despite this big news, he had made the decision to join the Marines. In fact, the reason he was late for the interview was that he had just come from their recruiting office in Oakland.

My mind was reeling. We sat in silence for a few moments, just breathing. Levar had grown up a ward of the court. At 18 and on the cusp of high school graduation, he was about to be, in every sense of the word, on his own. Young people moving from dependence to independence need loving adults to guide, counsel, and occasionally step in with concrete help. For those without parents, the transition into adulthood is a high-wire act performed without a safety net— and so often with depressingly predictable outcomes. No wonder an all-encompassing patriarchal system like the military seemed like an attractive option.

American Field Service, or AFS, came to mind. Started by a group of ambulance drivers just after World War II to support the goal of cross-cultural understanding, the well-known program gives high school kids the opportunity to live with a family in another country. Today AFS has expanded to include college-age students in year-abroad, family home stay programs. It felt right. "What do you think about a really big step this time?"

Instead of entering into a reassuring system that would also prove constricting, Levar went to Ecuador.

The year passed quickly and drew to a close; I knew that he had come home, but once again, I heard nothing. This ongoing pattern—being so present and then disappearing so precipitously—was hard on me—surely for him too. His telephone was again disconnected. I wrote him an urgent letter, but there was no response. With disappointment in my heart, I realized that the situation was out of my control. He would either show up or disappear forever. It was my job to do what I could, let go, and then…trust.

Two months later, Levar finally called. Could I meet him for lunch? Oh, yes, I certainly could!

I dropped everything and drove to Oakland. Sitting in the car, I watched him swinging down the street with an easy gait. He looked older, and there was a hand-woven pouch from South America slung over his shoulder. We headed off to a tiny Mexican restaurant down the street. When he ordered our lunch in fluent Spanish, the owner looked surprised.

"Before you say anything, Levar," I said, "I need to tell you how disappointed I felt when you didn't call." I felt myself sliding into that dangerous and unproductive place of blame and of "after all I've done for you" stuff, but I couldn't help myself.

He listened calmly without interrupting, an echo of our first interview. Finally, he said, "Do you want to hear what happened in Ecuador?"

In Ecuador, I encountered a family who couldn't communicate. Not because of the language, but because of their own walls. Somehow, being with people who had their own problems communicating helped me feel like I could begin trying to open up about who I was.

Six months passed. There was no heartfelt response from anyone in the family, despite my trying. So I worked harder. I took my brothers to soccer games, even though I hated soccer. I went to the open-air markets with my mother and learned never to argue with an Indian woman, because it would mean you'd be stuck there for hours! I scraped up my hands cutting and installing windows with my father. I learned all about the word, guantes. . .gloves.

In the end, they broke down their walls and opened up to each other. My father said that he loved us, me included, a feat that most South American men never accomplish. My brother told me it was a first time ever for their family. This changed the way I thought about myself, what I was truly capable of. Not only could I do good things for myself, I could let what I was learning ripple out into the world.

Compassion, empathy, gratitude: those qualities are what heal personal wounds and create happier lives. Just as I was basking in this amazing story and his amazing success and determination to give back, Levar's voice changed, hardened.

"Then I came home." He paused and continued. "I wanted to stand on my own, to prove to myself I could do it. It felt like I would be cheating if I kept running to you. My mom had quit her job again, so there wasn't any money. My brother was selling drugs. They all expected me to help them out, to bring in some money, and I didn't want to let them down." Levar didn't look me in the eye. "So I've been selling. Last week, I sold to a guy who turned out to be an undercover cop. He started to come after me, but I jumped on my bicycle and managed to get away." He finally looked up at me. "Don't worry, he doesn't know me and it's easy to stop." There were tears in his eyes. "That's when I called you."

"Why did you give up on yourself up like that, Levar?"

"My mom and my brother expected me to bring in money. I didn't know what else to do."

"That's not what I'm talking about."

Levar looked at me expectantly.

"I wonder if you got afraid after doing so well in Ecuador." He looked blank. "You've lived overseas for an entire year, you've returned speaking Spanish fluently, and your ability to concentrate is better than ever. You achieved the amazing feat of getting into your first choice college, and you're supposed to leave in January. Yet you were ready to throw that all away."

"Yeah, I guess I can be great anywhere except in my own neighborhood." Then, with characteristic honesty, he added, "The negativity pulls me down. I hear my mother doing drugs in the next room, and I get so low."

"But why does it feel like asking for help is a sign of weakness rather than strength?"

"Talking about it now, I know it isn't. But in the middle of everything...after depending on foster care and welfare and all that for so long, I just wanted to be independent. I didn't want to lean on anybody. And I've changed so much, done so much, I just needed to be on my own and get away." He hesitated. "Especially from you."

Frustration welled up again. He clung so tightly to the people who hurt him, while pushing away those who tried to help. I also saw how caught he was in the old negative belief, understandable in the light of all his instability, that everyone would leave him. Including me. Easier to leave first than wait for that painful and inevitable rejection. Levar continued: "Maybe I can write about this someday, you know, the story of my life."

"Don't you think your book will be more compelling if you keep going rather than quit?"

"Yes. But it's hard. I'm afraid you think I can't do it."

All the compassion and love I had for this boy rose up inside me in a giant wave. "Where did you ever get the idea that I'm going to give up on you? You're going to Morehouse on your feet or in a casket. And let me assure you, it will be fine with me either way." He laughed.

As we ate some of the best enchiladas I'd ever had, he showed me the photos from his trip, including shots of him with a beautiful German girlfriend in the Galapagos Islands.

It was time to go. I looked at him across the plastic tablecloth splashed with huge turquoise and red flowers. It occurred to me that being brave enough to try a different life so far from home had stripped him of his defenses. The thick walls he had built to protect him had finally fallen, leaving him more vulnerable than ever. Maybe he needed some other kind of safeguard. "How about you working in the Summer Search office for the next four months before you leave?" I asked. "I need the help, and you need the cash."

He looked interested, and then apprehensive. "I don't know how to type."

"You can learn. You'll need it for school anyway."

And so Levar came to work at Summer Search, navigating the two-hour bus commute from his world to mine. He settled in quickly and was soon making a real contribution in an increasingly busy office. He was especially helpful in talking to the often frightened new students—explaining, reassuring, and supporting.

Just a month before he was due to leave for Morehouse, a television producer named Judy Shills called. She was starting a new TV show, *The Diary Project*, to highlight the lives of high-risk high school students through their own diary entries. She wanted to document how writing helped overcome deprivation. Was there a Summer Search student who might participate?

I was skeptical, but Levar thought we should at least meet with her. When Judy came to the office, we were impressed with her integrity and enthusiasm, and Levar decided that we should agree to participate. He also wanted to volunteer to be the student interviewed.

Retelling and then rewriting his story again, this time with Judy, loosened the last layers of Levar's protective armor. He began to think new thoughts but some of them were "bad" thoughts. It began with violent dreams. He was beating someone up, viciously kicking them as they went down. He would wake up in a sweat, terrified. Growing up, anger had been a luxury he could not afford. As a young child, it brought instant and severe physical punishment. Later, in the foster homes, anger carried the risk of removal, and yet another new placement. Now, living with his mother again, anger could break the new and fragile bond that held them together.

I was convinced that Levar's habit of swallowing anger was one of the causes of his ongoing struggle with depression. I told him it was a good thing he was starting to feel mad, it meant he was getting better. But he needed outlets, safe outlets. I wanted him to start lifting weights, running, and to keep talking: to Judy, to me, to anyone who would listen. All that negativity was ready to—needed to—come to the surface.

Judy wanted to film Levar in the neighborhood where he had spent his earliest days, the infamous Acorn Projects of West Oakland. He courageously agreed to revisit the place where he and his brothers watched their mother's downward slide into addiction, despair, and finally homelessness. On the day scheduled for filming, the crew waited for several hours for him to arrive. Just as they started packing up, he appeared. That morning, old memories of being taken away from all he knew and placed into foster care had risen up inside him. It took a long time for him to get out of bed.

They finished filming the segment. As they were wrapping up, Judy mentioned she wanted to meet his mother someday. "How about now?" Levar said spontaneously. They drove together to the nursing home nearby where she worked as an aide.

Joann's initial response to *The Diary Project* had been negative: "Those white people are just using you." But today she willingly engaged with Judy in a conversation about those traumatic early years, when she struggled and failed to take care of her family. "You know," she said, "I treat the strangers here today better than I treated my own children." Then to Levar's astonishment, she agreed to be filmed as part of the project.

Examining the past was a big risk for both Levar and his mother. As they talked, bringing to the surface the memories and traumas that had been off limits for so long, Levar learned more details about his mother's childhood. The youngest in a family of eight children, with an alcoholic mother and an incarcerated father, she hit the streets at 13. Then she too became a ward of the court. At 21, Joann became pregnant. From this new vantage point, on the cusp of adulthood, Levar could see her not just as the mother who failed him, but the young girl who was herself failed during her own childhood.

Ultimately, *The Diary Project* was never broadcast, but for Levar and his mother, it didn't matter. The opportunity to talk about the past allowed them to start anew. Their courage to venture into unexplored territory, the shame that had for years been locked up in a vault of guilt and sorrow, opened their hearts. Forgiveness flooded in, only this time without the burden of remorse they had shouldered for so long.

Today Joann has much to be proud of. She has been clean and sober for 16 years and has had stable work at the nursing home for the past 10. After 20 years on the streets, she now has her own apartment and is a loving grandparent to her oldest son's children. When Levar comes to the Bay Area, he stays with her and looks forward to sharing his new life that hopefully will include a family and children too.

* * *

A few days before his departure for Morehouse, Levar and I were working in companionable silence in the office. I was working on this book, and one afternoon, stuck, I showed him a few pages and asked him if he thought I was missing something. He replied, "Yes. You don't speak to the real power behind what you do."

"What's that?"

"The fact that you love me no matter what I do."

"Oh."

"In the foster homes, they cared for me only when I behaved." He paused and added, "I'm scared to go to Morehouse, but I know that if I don't do well there, you will still love me."

"I'm not so sure about that."

Levar interrupted me, smiling. "Of course, you will be disappointed. But I know you will still love me." He looked at me intently and added, "You keep asking me what I've learned coming to work in the office. I used to think it was just me, but now I see that you love every student that way. That's why we try so hard for you."

A rush of feelings made my eyes sting. It was true, I did love these kids. Summer Search, which began as a simple idea that came from observing my own children grow in their own summer programs, was now in truth something else entirely. It was the coming together of all that I had ever felt and ever done: the pain I experienced in my own childhood, my understanding of addiction through my father's struggles, my interest in psychiatric nursing, my husband Pierre's stories about his life-changing experiences in India as a young man. All of it, all of it had come together and brought me to this wonderful place of understanding. Yet it was more. To love Levar, to love them—all of them—was to feel broader, bigger, to go far beyond my own little life.

So many people, students and staff, who are now attracted to Summer Search, experience this opportunity and begin to expand their own lives, to transcend their own limited circles of compassion. Levar and I looked at each other for a long moment, gratitude flooding our hearts.

* * *

Yet transitions are never easy. As the time came to leave for Morehouse, the expectations on Levar as "the bright one with a future," became increasingly hard to bear. His mother had not gone beyond the seventh grade, and his two brothers, who hadn't graduated from high school, had been in and out of prison. The pressure caused him to withdraw. His financial aid forms, filled out inaccurately, were rejected. He told me he had called the admissions department over and over, and only got a recording. I discovered he was calling in the late afternoon, long after office hours in Atlanta.

We finally contacted the financial aid department. Magically, new forms arrived and we filled them out together. When I asked him why he had tried to sabotage himself again, Levar reverted to his old behavior. "I think my family just quits when the going gets tough. You know there was only one role model that did well, my uncle, but he dropped out of college his last semester. I guess it was just too hard."

"Levar, damn it, think! We've been over this again and again. The last semester? Your uncle quit not because it was too hard, but because he was going to be too successful. He could not shake the negative messages from his past. Success is scary. You know what failure is like. So does your mom. It's predictable. For all of us, what's predictable, even when it is destructive, is what's safe. You don't have a clue about what will happen to you in college; that is, of course, unless you plan on shooting yourself in the foot again and doing poorly."

Levar smiled. After that, his face was more relaxed and there was a brighter look in his eyes. The uneasiness and disorientation he felt about going off to college was finally fully on the table. He now knew why he was afraid. "Linda, no matter how far I climb, there is still that foster child in me. Every step forward reaffirms that loss and that sense of being discarded and out of step with the rest of the world."

But it was time to stop making excuses. From now on, it didn't matter that he came from the projects and grew up in foster care. It was up to him to either build on what he had gained, or to give in to his background of trauma and loss. This next step was his chance to create a new identity, not through fantasy trips with Summer Search, but on his own terms. The choice was clear.

It was Levar's last day at the office. There wasn't much left to say. We slipped out for a quick lunch, and the conversation drifted. When we returned to the office, Levar looked around and said, "I'm going to miss this place."

I could feel my throat tightening. "Don't get me started. Let's just finish up, and I'll drop you off at the bus stop." We hurried to clean up and close things down for the Christmas holiday. Finally, it was time to go. On the way, I fussed. "Remember to get gloves, *guantes.* It'll be cold there."

"Yeah."

"And be careful, there's still lots of racism in Georgia."

"I'll be careful." He turned and gave me a long look and then a quick hug. As he stepped out of the car, he leaned down, looking through the open window, his head cocked at an angle, waiting.

I leaned over too, looking up at him. I wanted to say one last thing, hopefully something profound, or at least something he could carry with him for a long time. Blinking back the tears, I said, "Don't forget to be a good investment."

He laughed. With tears in his eyes, too, there was one last huge smile, a wave, and then he was gone.

* * *

Levar's initial experience on campus at Morehouse was jarring. For some reason he thought the men at Morehouse would be poor and struggling just like him. He had no experience with black men from upper-class or even middle-class backgrounds. At Morehouse, he met young men who were second- and third-generation students. The stability and confidence they exuded was strange and at first hard to understand.

In his junior year, Levar did indeed become a good investment by making the dean's list. Then two dreams came true. In 2000, he met Oprah as he was selected as one of the Oprah Winfrey Scholars, a competitive merit-based scholarship for students with strong academic records, a history of community service, and clear financial need. He also went to Africa that same year on an academic scholarship through the University of Cape Town.

And so in 2002 Levar graduated. A young man from foster care and the projects graduated. I was there.

And yet, to what? In spite of his enormous achievements there was still no real extended network of support and very little applause.

After a year of hesitation Levar applied and was accepted to Miami University in Ohio for his PhD in political science. As completion neared the heights he had reached were seeming to backfire—he was in debt and old problems with concentration reappeared—blocking his work on his dissertation. One morning he called me panicky and asked if he could come to my home in the Bay Area to have a quiet place to write. The PhD program at Miami University was closing down the following year and he was one of three students. In the room designated for them to work, there were three chairs—two were suddenly empty. Gone. His decade-long dream of becoming a professor at Morehouse depended on finishing that dissertation.

In a moment of uneasiness, I told him I would do anything to help him—if he needed to come back to the Bay Area, of course, he could use the guest house to write.

No word for a month. Then Levar emailed me back saying that for the first time in 23 years, I had given him bad advice. He needed to figure it out on his own rather than run away. Of course, he was right.

I didn't know what was going to happen but all I could do is wait. Would the risk to stay tight in a bud finally become more painful than the risk to blossom? I emailed Levar one last time—any news?

Good afternoon, men of Morehouse. I am definitely where I need to be after all the hard work, sacrifice, and toil. My name is Levar Lamar Smith and I am your professor for Political Science 285. It has been a long journey to return back to Morehouse as a professor given that it felt like an unreachable dream when I was a student here in 2002. I am grateful for the hard lessons. I hope that my passion and drive to succeed along with my commitment to teaching will inspire you in your own personal journey to also reach higher, go beyond, and eventually give back.

Gentlemen, let us begin.

ten

Flipping the Script: Carlton

A man's value is not measured by the years he has lived or even the work he has done. A man's value is measured by the character he has molded.
—Robert Browning

While Levar, Myra, David, and so many others were struggling and triumphing, Jay and Katherine had been working hard too, making their mark on Summer Search.

Jay recruited an excellent board of directors, including a passionate board president, Fredi Stevenson. He found a tiny office in Boston and began recruiting students right away. At first the summer programs were worried about accepting students not interviewed by me, but they were soon reassured. The Boston Summer Search students also performed well on their challenging trips, and returned home to rewrite their stories and think new thoughts.

Katherine and I settled in and began expanding the Bay Area program. She was concerned about Summer Search seniors: "What about college counseling?" she asked. It was a good idea—and I encouraged her to go ahead and start a program for our seniors.

New people and new talent helped me think new thoughts as well. In my reading, I came across an idea that would prove helpful in the years ahead: "Since kindergarten we are taught to focus on our weaknesses," said Harvard Business School professor and Fredi's husband, Howard Stevenson, quoted in Eric Sinoway's book, *Howard's Gift*. He continued, "This constant focus on what needs improving rather than on what comes naturally, requires a huge investment of intellectual and emotional energy. All of us have a plethora of weaknesses but relatively few strengths. By moving our focus away from where we struggle to where we excel, we can leverage our energy towards greater mastery and more success."

This reminded me of the countless hours I spent helping my children focus on areas that were hard for them, while often neglecting what they did well. I felt lucky to come across this powerful idea when I did; I was soon to interview a student whose many deficits defined him almost completely.[1]

Jay had flown in from Boston the night before and was joining me for an exciting day of interviewing. We both headed off to meet with our ever-faithful referring teacher, Jan Hudson. After a long career in schools with high-risk students, Jan was experienced in understanding the needs of kids from severely impoverished backgrounds. She had recently become vice principal at Mission High, in the heart of the Latino district in San Francisco, after Wilson—Solaria's school and Jan's former employer—shut down.

When I first went to Mission High, in spite of the dignified building—spacious hallways lined with beautiful handmade tiles

---

1. Sinoway, Eric C. and Merrill Meadow: *Howard's Gift: Uncommon Wisdom to Inspire Your Life's Work*, New York: St. Martin's Press. 2012.

and high ceilings crowned by majestic wooden arches—it was a dirty, chaotic place, and the atmosphere was one of futility. Soon after, the administrative team changed, and Jan came on board as vice principal. Lupe Arabolos, an efficient woman with a warm smile and an even warmer heart, became the new principal. In just two years, to everyone's surprise, Mission High became a place that fostered hope rather than despair. Watching this transformation made me realize how closely linked the climate and performance of every school is to its leadership.

When Jay and I arrived at her office, Jan told us that she had eight students ready to be interviewed, but that there was one in particular she was especially eager for us to evaluate. She paused and looked out the window before turning and looking straight into our eyes. "Linda, he's 18 years old and just a sophomore here. I'd say he is barely literate; maybe he can read at the fourth-grade level. His history is grim. He grew up in Sacramento, and as a young child he was seriously abused; both his vision and hearing were damaged when he was thrown out a window."

Jay and I winced. Jan nodded and continued. "I know this is hard. At 13 or maybe 14, he was on the streets in Sacramento selling drugs before getting shot and ending up in the juvenile court system. His name, by the way, is Carlton. He is now living with an older brother."

Jan looked at both of us again before concluding, "I know what you're thinking. He doesn't sound like Summer Search material—"

"Jan," I interrupted, "it's not just Summer Search material. I've been reading about language development in young children. By age three, low-income kids only have half the words that middle-class kids do. This significantly impacts their eventual IQ as well as their ability to think abstractly. As you know, kids who have trouble with abstract thinking don't do very well in Summer Search. That, combined with the probable multiple learning disabilities this boy must have, makes me worry. He certainly doesn't need another failure or rejection in his life."

Jan replied, "At first that's what I thought too. But in 28 years of working with inner-city kids, I've never seen a boy with this much deficit who"—she paused and her face flushed—"is still trying." She looked off in the distance again and then added softly, "I think you should, at least, take a look."

As we prepared for a long day of interviewing, Jay and I talked about Carlton. Jan's description said a lot about his character, but was character enough to overcome such extreme deficit? Our goal was to identify kids who at least had some chance of rising above, which almost always meant going to college. Was it fair to create those expectations in an 18-year-old sophomore who couldn't read beyond the fourth-grade level?

While we were waiting for Carlton, Jay asked, "What was that study you mentioned to Jan? What were the actual IQs of those kids?"

It's older, 1995, but I'm finding it relevant in our work. Two psychologists from the University of Kansas discovered that the way parents and caregivers talked to children had a significant impact on that child's IQ. They showed that the achievement gap as evidenced by the famed 30 million word gap between low-income and higher-income children begins in the earliest years of life and can be measured by the age of three.[2]

"It's fascinating Jay," I replied leaning forward as I continued. "For middle-class kids the average IQ was 117 and for low-income children it was 79. It seems that talking to young children has a huge impact on who they will eventually become." I thought for a minute. "I wonder about our emphasis on kids talking to us?"

---

2. Hart, Betty and Todd R. Risley. *Meaningful Differences in the Everyday Experience of Young American Children.* Baltimore: P.H. Brookes, 1995.

At this point Carlton burst through the half open door. Tall, thin, and dressed in the standard baggy costume of oversized pants and shirt, he took a seat, lanky limbs sticking out at all angles. I noticed that his body moved with the elasticity of a rubber band. Looking at us he stuck out his hand, shook our hands, and cracked a joke with a confidence that bordered on bravado. He was late and he was loud. Whatever educational deficits this boy had, he certainly had people skills.

Then Jay and I glanced at his essay and saw two tortured paragraphs written in a shaky scrawl. When I told Carlton we wanted to know what it was like to be in his shoes, he began to squirm in his chair. After a few attempts at changing the subject, he gave in and took the plunge.

"Okay. There are seven of us, three boys and four girls." He paused. "Actually, I haven't seen too much of my family. My mother was always incarcerated." He looked at me then Jay to confirm that we understood what that meant. "You know, in and out of jail," he emphasized. "My father, well, he's someone who leaves for 15 years and doesn't call or write."

We sat, listening. Carlton looked at me angrily. "Why should I go looking for someone who's not looking for me?" There was certain logic to this. I nodded. "Anyway, my mother got married again after I was born, but no one was there for me. My stepfather was always working, and my mom was never there. I had no one to look up to, no one to play catch with, no one to tuck me in at night and tell me a bedtime story. I was mad at the world, you know?"

He paused to catch his breath, then looked out the window. He dropped his head and said quietly, "Everyone has a mother. Who was I supposed to send a Mother's Day card to? My mom in jail? Ha!" he concluded, strangely triumphant. Then, as an afterthought, he added more calmly, "My life was full of broken promises."

I glanced at Jay, momentarily unsure of what to do. Carlton didn't seem to notice. "Let me tell you what else happened," he said. "I have this uncle. When I was five, I still liked to play around a lot. You know? Anyway, one day he was crazy drunk, and he banged me against the wall and then threw me out the window: brain damage, ear damage, sight damage. My uncle got what he deserved…he went to jail. But what about me?"

This was hard to hear. Carlton somehow sensed I was not quite giving him my full attention, and looked at me closely before continuing. "My stepfather kicked me out of the house when I was 15. After that, I lived on the street. I spent 12 weeks at Juvenile Hall for car theft, possession of marijuana, and resisting arrest. Man, I went through a lot of disrespect. After two months, I was back out on probation. I had to go to school and get good grades, or they would send me back to jail. But I had no place to live, so how was I going to make money to live on?"

He took a deep breath. "So I went back to selling drugs. One night, I was claiming the colors, and figured I'd get me a few sales. Wrong place…wrong time…wrong everything. A drive-by shooting hit me in the back, and I ended up in the hospital for three weeks." Pausing again for just a few seconds, as though to digest what he had just said, or maybe just to catch his breath he continued more calmly. "When I got out, I called my brother here in San Francisco. I figured I wasn't going to be alive for very long in Sacramento, you know, so I came on down here."

The whole picture—severe abuse and neglect, learning disabilities, limited vocabulary, in all likelihood a lower-than-average IQ, and surely an unclear sense of right and wrong—seemed to indicate that no matter how charismatic this boy was, he wouldn't be able to take advantage of the kinds of challenges Summer Search offered.

Then I remembered Jan's words about character, and that in spite of those massive deficiencies, he was still trying. I wondered about taking a risk, but first I needed to know about his values or, as I would say to another counselor, his super-ego development. "Carlton, you've done a good job here today, but these issues you're bringing up are serious. I'm going to simplify all this complicated information and put our final decision about whether Summer Search is the right program for you on just one last question. Okay? So here we go: just one quick roll of the dice."

Carlton sucked in his breath and rolled his eyes.

I took a deep breath too. "You've had a tough time, Carlton. I understand you've had to do many difficult things to survive." I waited, but he just looked at me blankly. "Here's my question, and please answer as honestly as you can." Carlton was starting to fidget in his chair again. I looked at him intently, and said, "What is the worst thing you've ever done?"

Carlton twisted his mouth then closed his eyes. For the first time in the interview, he paused. Then he dropped his head and said quietly, "I never killed anyone." There was a momentary silence before he raised his head and looked at me squarely. "I did have to beat people up, but I never took no pleasure in it."

Our eyes locked. I exhaled. Regardless of the brutality of his childhood, Carlton had emerged with a sense of right and wrong. Although he had to do terrible things to get by, he had somehow held on to a fragile sense of ethics. This boy deserved our allegiance and compassion and, in spite of my reservations, the chance to join Summer Search.

I told Carlton he was in, an announcement he accepted with surprising calm. I wondered if, as with many survivors of abuse, he had learned to read people so well that he had already sensed my thoughts. I began thinking about what program to choose for him.

Clearly, he needed academic help, but the academic programs we worked with were for high-achievers. Unsure what to do, I started telling him about a possible wilderness expedition. "Yes, ma'am," he interrupted, "but I surely do need to get me some credits, some summer school or something."

He was right on that one. His focus was firmly fixed, understandably, on his deficits and wounds. "Hey, Carlton," I said, "I do have another question for you. What are your strong points?" His face took on a blank look. Then he shook his head, puzzled. Here was a question he had no ready answer for. Finally, he just shrugged.

"What about Wolfeboro?" Jay said.

Carlton and I both jumped. We had forgotten about him.

"What's Wolfeboro?" I asked.

Jay continued talking, "Carlton, you probably have severe learning differences that have never been diagnosed. Wolfeboro is a school in New Hampshire that helps kids who have trouble learning. I don't know much about it yet, but I'll find out."

I felt a momentary twinge. How is it that Jay knew about a program I had never heard of?

A few days later, back in Boston, Jay did more research and discovered that the director of Wolfeboro, a man named Bill Cooper, was coming to San Francisco in two weeks to meet families who could afford the six-week tuition—a staggering $6,000. Katherine, Carlton, and I made an appointment to meet with him.

Bill was a conservative-looking, middle-aged man in a suit and bow tie. "Breakfast begins promptly at 7:50," he told us, describing the rigors of the program. "No one is ever late." Carlton looked incredulous, and cut his eyes at Katherine and me. Bill looked straight at him. "Actually, a person might be late once, but then that's it. It never happens again." There was a long pause; none of us knew quite what to say.

"You ask why?" Bill looked at our uncomprehending faces as we managed to nod obediently in unison. "Imagine arriving at a big dining hall with 300 people standing quietly by their chairs, waiting. They all turn to look at you as you walk in the door. Late. You see, no one can sit down for breakfast until everyone is present."

As this information sank in, Bill went on to describe the small classes with just four students to each teacher. The day's lessons didn't stop until every student mastered the material. Carlton began to ask a series of nervous questions. "What if I don't get it? Will they yell at me? How can they wait for just me?" Then a final anguished plea, "What if I can't get it?"

Bill told Carlton not to worry. The teachers would go over the materials after class with him until each day's lesson was learned. There were two classes every morning and one after lunch. Afternoons were for sports, and then there was one hour of free time. Every night after dinner there was a three-hour study hall with a monitor. Six rigorous days a week.

Carlton couldn't fathom following that kind of strict routine, nor could he believe Bill's reassurance that, no matter how severe his learning problems, he would succeed at Wolfeboro. Listening to his fears, understandable in the face of the terrible physical, psychological, and emotional damage he had suffered at home and in school, made Katherine and me more determined. Yet as we looked across the table at each other, we saw the same concern—would it be possible for Carlton to succeed given the severity of his handicaps?

Bill looked at Carlton, who was again squirming in his chair, and asked if he had any last questions or worries. Carlton hesitated, but finally said, "I don't think there are any people of color out there."

"We have some," Bill answered quickly. To our surprise, he turned the projector on again and flipped through several slides. Twice he said, "See, there's one!"

Carlton, Katherine, and I looked at each other soberly. It was a moment of uncomfortable familiarity. *So what,* we read in each other's eyes, *let it go.* Bill seemed open to helping Carlton, and that was what we wanted.

Bill was already moving on. He was willing to take a risk and offer Carlton a scholarship, even though he was concerned that the program might be too restrictive for a student from such a troubled background.

We were concerned too. Carlton's whole life had been so chaotic. He had never done the same thing at the same time or had any kind of rhythm or routine. Yes, he was in school, sort of, but his inner-city schools were also chaotic and he was often absent. As I closed my eyes, I could see his athletic body, bobbing and weaving through streets and alleys, tense, vigilant, ready to respond to the emergency of the moment.

It was going to be a big risk. But we would do everything we needed to do to get Carlton ready. Bill requested he be tested for hearing and sight, and arrive with new glasses and a hearing aid. Since he was on Medi-Cal and in special programs at school, we thought this would be no problem. It took three months.

Testing of any kind had always meant bad news, so Carlton avoiding making the appointments. Then, finally, after threats from Katherine, he met with a counselor for an evaluation. A new hearing aid was fitted, but the glasses barely helped him. It turned out Medi-Cal had simply refilled an old prescription because the new one was more expensive. With three weeks left, Katherine told Carlton, "Throw those damned things in the garbage can! Give me the prescription, and we'll pay for it."

When he put on his new glasses, Carlton was ecstatic. He could see! When he called with a jubilant thank you, Katherine said, "Carlton, what's the point of sending you off on a $6,000 scholarship if you can't see and you can't hear?" Carlton laughed, but not too hard. After a lifetime of navigating danger, he was all too aware that in leaving his life of negativity he was about to take a positive step: the biggest risk of all.

The first two weeks passed without any news. Then one morning, the luxurious stillness of the office in summer time was interrupted by a collect call. An almost unintelligible voice on the line howled, "Get me out of here!"

"Is there a problem, Carlton?" I asked calmly, but I could feel my heartbeat accelerating.

"Damn right, there's a problem. You don't understand, Linda, there is no room here; I can't breathe. I'm going to blow up!" After ranting for about 20 minutes, Carlton suddenly said, "Okay, I'll stay one more week. That's it." He hung up abruptly. The calls continued once or twice a week over the following month, each echoing the familiar pattern: rant followed by an abrupt hang-up.

After the first call, I worried that it was over. Then I started to grow less worried. Carlton was finding the way to stick with it by making a resilient choice to reach out and put his distress into words instead of withdrawing or lashing out. This was new behavior, and a huge step on his part. By making those choices and turning that corner, Katherine and I felt he was headed toward completing the biggest and maybe even the first significant success of his life.

Yet completion and success were new; mistakes and failure were familiar. With one week to go, Carlton made a bad judgment call. Late for class, he took a shortcut and used the staff bathroom. A teacher found him there and got right up in his face. In his face! Schooled on the street, Carlton's boundaries were severely tested.

"He had no right to disrespect me like that. I admit I shouldn't have used their bathroom, but he has to apologize!"

Think fast, I told myself, *this could escalate*. As casually as I could, I said, "Why not use the Robin Williams approach?"

"What?" I could tell Carlton was confused. I waited. He finally bit. "Okay. Who's Robin Williams?"

"Robin Williams, you know, the actor and comedian. Well, Robin says the best thing to do in a case like this is…Carlton, are you listening?"

"I'm listening, but I don't see your point."

"Let me repeat what Robin Williams would say. Are you listening?"

"Yes."

"Let…the asshole…have…the…last…word."

A quiet chuckle. "Okay. I get it."

* * *

When Carlton arrived home, he came with many certificates and awards. The one he was proudest of was "Most Improved Student," signed by the boss man himself, Mr. Cooper. When he called into the office, Katherine and I both jumped on the phone.

"I tell you, it was a shock. For a person with my disabilities, you know, a kid from the inner city, I had a lot of anxiety. I felt like I didn't fit in up there. So, at first, I sort of put up an attitude. That's when I met the dean of students, Mr. Oreo. Can you believe that name? Anyway he had a military background and was sort of the enforcer, you know, when things go wrong, you see him."

Carlton paused. "The kids, well, like I said, I didn't fit in. At first it seemed that we didn't have anything in common. But midway on the camping trip, it was really cold and wet. I started asking if I could help, stuff like carry extra weight. We sort of started talking and, what do you know? We became friends. And the classes, whew! I must say they were really intense, but I kinda adapted to it."

Katherine said, "Carlton, that's what we admire about you—you keep reaching out."

He chuckled appreciatively, then continued with real energy. "Let me tell you about my reading comprehension class. It was the first time I ever saw an almanac. It was really fun." He paused. "Only one thing. I just hated the fact it was so quiet. In my schools there's always something going on."

"The academics were weird. Usually in school, I watch the other kids, you know, just shadow. When I don't get it, I just fall asleep, right at my desk. People knew. I couldn't get even the simplest things. When they tried to help me, I still didn't get it, so they would get mad. So I just shut down."

The tone in Carlton's voice abruptly changed, softened. "But, you know, no one put me down there. No one got mad or frustrated at Wolfeboro. They would keep explaining it in different ways until I understood. Yet I still brought all the negativity I felt from all those years in school. I would get mad, but then I saw it wasn't them. It wasn't them...*it was on me*."

Katherine and I looked at each other. We both had tears in our eyes as Carlton continued. "With other programs, you get tested first and then they put you into smart, intermediate, and then, well, slow. *For the first time I was just as smart as them.* So, like I said, if things were going to change, *it was on me*."

He had discovered he was smart. Carlton could also, after that initial shock of not fitting in, recognize what he needed to do to make his time at Wolfeboro successful. Katherine and I looked at each other again and smiled. If only all of us could see that we are so often our own greatest enemy. Yes, indeed, if only everyone could take Carlton's attitude about changing: "*It's on me*."

For the Fall Event, we decided to ask Carlton to give a speech, the first of his life. He was eager for the challenge, but he needed help.

Katherine went to his school for several afternoons and listened to him speak out loud while she wrote down the words. Gradually, with Katherine's coaching, he developed an excellent presentation.

Carlton, when not forced to focus on his weaknesses, was able for the first time to see his actual strengths. To our surprise and his, he memorized his words rather easily. We only worried about one thing: his tendency to improvise!

On the night of the Fall Event, as he faced the audience in a tie and a stylish vest cut from some kind of paisley material, Carlton's face broke into a colossal smile. I felt a rush of panic. In spite of Katherine's dire warnings not to deviate from the script, I was sure he was going to get carried away. This speech could last a long time. The smile broadened, I closed my eyes, and Carlton began.

"My worst nightmare started on June 27th, 1996. I was on my way to some place called New Hampshire, where I didn't know anyone, and breakfast was every day at 7:50. It was the first time I ever was on an airplane. But the greatest shock was when I got there. There aren't that many black people in New Hampshire. In my program, there were only four, in the whole camp—and they were all on the kitchen staff!"

The audience laughed in delight. Carlton went on to describe the rigors of a set schedule with increasing enthusiasm. "Can you imagine doing the same thing every day, all day?"

By the end, he was almost hugging the microphone. And despite the clear temptation to roam, he stuck with his memorized speech almost to the word.

"When I first got there, I acted like I usually do. You know, talking back, being late, acting tough. That did not work! Excuses were not accepted! I saw I'd have to rearrange, you know, flip the script. I understood I was there to learn, and that going home was not an option. Whew! And, boy did I learn! I learned math and reading, two grades worth! I have never done anything so hard in my entire life." The smile broadened, "I did not quit."

Just like Jan said, I thought to myself.

"No, I didn't quit, because there were people who believed in me, who wanted me to get through that program and people who had worked to get me there. So tonight I want to tell you all, never quit. Never ever quit! Set a goal in life and achieve it. If I can do it, so can you."

Afterward, while Katherine and I watched, people surrounded Carlton, shaking his hand and wishing him well. His colossal smile stayed put all evening long.

That spring, Carlton sent his report card to us by mail. His senior year at Mission, he had made the honor roll. When Katherine and I opened it tenderly, it seemed as precious and unlikely a document as we could possibly imagine. We put it on the refrigerator door in the Summer Search office. He was going to be the first in his family to graduate from high school, a true trailblazer, breaking entrenched multi-generational patterns of poverty and educational failures. We all beamed.

Yet, in the face of such accomplishments, it was too easy for all of us to forget the reality of the big picture. For students like Carlton, who have not been nurtured or have had a supportive childhood, graduation from high school, a potent symbol of the end of childhood, is a particularly precarious time. Being expected to move on, let go of the childhood they actually never had, can become a threat, not a celebration. For some kids, this developmental crisis is so overwhelming that they drop out and don't graduate—a poignant attempt to avoid a transition they are psychologically incapable of making.

Carlton was going to need ongoing and abundant support in this vulnerable moment. Hearing that his graduation day was going to be a big event, with many family members in attendance, was heartening. Maybe coming together to support Carlton's success would be a new beginning for them, too.

But, as the big day got closer, the excuses started rolling in. One by one, his sister, then his aunt, and finally his stepfather were too busy to come. Even the person who had helped him the most, his brother, indicated he might have to work. This often happens in families who haven't achieved many traditional markers of success, but Katherine and I were still furious. It was Carlton's first major triumph in life. How could they leave him hanging? For his part,

Carlton was convinced that, surely, they would change their minds, find a way at the last minute.

A few weeks passed, and then one early morning the phone rang. "Linda, are you coming to my graduation?"

"Of course, I'm planning on it. What time is it?"

"In two hours."

"Carlton! You told me Friday. Katherine and I had no idea it was today! We have more than a hundred kids about to go off on their trips—kids who forgot equipment, ordered wrong airline tickets, or are in some kind of trouble. I just can't. I'm sorry."

There was a heavy silence on the other end of the line. My heart clenched. "But you know I'm always with you in spirit," I said, hating the words even before they came out of my mouth.

There was a long pause. Finally, in a small voice he asked, "Is it possible for me to speak to Katherine, please?"

Katherine listened quietly. I heard her ask, "What time?" Then, suddenly, she was gone. I began to visualize her with bags of fatigue under her eyes, in her blue jeans, dropping everything to grab a disposable camera and head toward Mission High. I could see her at the gym, crawling over decades of encrusted chewing gum and dried spit, to get the perfect shot of Carlton coming up on stage. And Jan Hudson, the referring teacher, getting the perfect shot of them both.

So Carlton, unheralded, unnoticed, and undermined (again) by his family, against all odds, graduated from high school. Although his family wasn't there, one exhausted, devoted, wholehearted young woman was, and that was enough. Carlton had his witness, he had his pictures, and he had Katherine. Now he could go on to make this success truly his own.

But what was he going on to do? He still struggled with reading and finding the discipline to follow a schedule on his own with any degree of consistency; Katherine and I worried about the next step. We both knew something more was needed to prevent Carlton from drifting toward an aimless, or worse, criminal life.

Carlton told us that military recruiters had approached him. At that vulnerable moment, joining a structured program that would take care of him seemed like a decent idea, but he was worried, with good reason, about passing the physical. His hearing and vision problems were serious. Then there was the written exam, and Carlton still panicked when taking tests. We didn't know what to do other than to listen and then urge him to, at least, give it a try.

Then he disappeared. Katherine tried to reach him, but his usually reliable pager was disconnected. Three months later, he finally checked in, apologetic and vague. He brushed off our questions with talk of "family problems." But he had lots of news. He was working part-time at the Y, and the kids loved him! He had found a counselor who would help him get enrolled in a special program at a local junior college. But he also wanted to keep his options open. Would Katherine go with him to the Army recruiting office?

He was so optimistic that, all of a sudden, we were hopeful as well.

Yet none of these plans panned out. His work at the Y remained off and on with no real direction or possibility of benefits. After hesitating, he finally took the written exam for the Army, but tests of any kind brought excruciating and incapacitating anxiety, and his scores were too low. At the junior college, in a special program for low-achievers, he was the only English speaker. He came to see us at the office, and we listened to him describe the walls closing in on him. "It also feels like I'm getting dumber and dumber," he concluded.

The answer to how Carlton found a way to overcome his limitations was a surprise to everyone, probably to himself most of all. It started with him dropping by the Summer Search office once a week to help with filing. Then he began to show up more often. Soon he created a niche for himself by running errands and taking care of office supplies. He assumed ownership of the many mailings. Before we knew it, he was indispensable, so we hired him full-time. His hours were flexible, which helped him slowly develop an internal sense of accountability.

When not under the pressure of the inevitable criticism and judgment that came with focusing on his weaknesses, his buried strengths continued to emerge. As his anxiety lessened, Carlton's ability to think clearly and work consistently began to improve dramatically. On Mondays, he would show up with lists of what he wanted to accomplish during the week. Almost magically, since it required both a written and a driving test—he got his driver's license. As he became more capable and confident, we decided to invest in a camera and have him videotape our events instead of freelancing the job out. This seemingly minor decision became a major turning point.

A commercial film production company, Winton Dupont, had offered to donate their services to update our outdated Summer Search recruitment video. I invited Carlton to go along with me to a series of meetings. Before long, he was meeting with the owner, Dave Winton, on his own. As their relationship grew, Dave started training Carlton in the mechanics of the film production business.

This unique chance to learn visually in a hands-on way was the beginning of a process that allowed Carlton to reach true mastery for the first time in his life. He reacted like a man who had found his first drink of cool water after a life of constant thirst. The universal deep human need to be effective, to be of value, was met for the first time. It was a fine thing to watch.

One day in late spring, a teacher from one of the roughest schools in the Bay Area—Castlemont, in East Oakland—called to ask if

Katherine or I could speak to a small group of students. We were both busy, and I was about to say no when Carlton walked by my desk. On impulse, I asked if he would like to go. He said yes.

The teacher told Katherine later that, as Carlton was addressing the group, two girls at the back of the room started fiddling with each other's hair. Without hesitating, Carlton said, "Ladies, this is not a beauty parlor, it's a classroom." The rest of the kids snapped to attention. Carlton's potentially crushing handicaps made him struggle with literacy, but focusing on his considerable people skills was helping him grow even stronger.

Gradually, this young man, who came from so little, started recruiting other students to Summer Search, kids who might never have had the courage to apply on their own. He understood that young people from severely limited environments had special issues; he knew how to talk to them and how to gain their trust. In his second year working for Summer Search, he got his first business card, his first raise, and the title to go with it: director of community outreach.

When it came time to recruit students from his former school, Mission High, I went with Carlton. He was dressed in a full suit and tie and looked unbelievably sharp. We passed two custodians in the hallway, and they looked at him with surprise and then with suspicion that seemed to border on resentment. This boy was not supposed to succeed. The afternoon passed quickly as he spoke to two groups of students and then played our new video. There were many enthusiastic kids, more than usual, and it was a satisfying moment. Packing up at the end of the day, we headed out to give a report to Jan Hudson. On our way a school counselor stepped out of his office and shouted out down the long, now empty hallway, "Hey, Carlton, you going to college?"

I turned and watched the color drain from Carlton's face. The look of satisfaction and triumph disappeared as his whole body crumpled.

We turned a corner. I hissed, "Carlton, don't you ever let someone do that to you again. Damn him. You say, 'Sure, I'm going to college.' What an asshole."

* * *

The process took 10 years, but his multiple experiences eventually gave Carlton a chance to deconstruct, rethink, and retell his story. Finally, he stopped listening to the messages he had received all his life: that he was incapable of learning and destined for a life of failure. Instead, he began to think new thoughts.

Carlton's story is a testimony to the transformative power of character, determination, and grit in overcoming severe disabilities and incapacitating anxieties. Vocabulary can be learned; IQ is far from carved in stone; confidence can be restored.

Carlton found the courage to leave Summer Search to start his own video production company. He married his longtime girlfriend and began creating what no one in his family had given him a blueprint for—a successful career and a happy family. Today he works with a video production company that sends him all over the world. At the time of this writing, he was filming in Dubai.

Told repeatedly that he would never make it in life, Carlton has indeed "flipped the script."

* * *

As for Katherine, Jay, and me? We have flipped the script as well. Jay, after successfully launching the first satellite office in Boston, went on to develop and lead a national expansion effort. Katherine then moved into my job and became an outstanding Executive Director of the San Francisco office. She left to start a family for a few years but has returned and continues to work half-time at Summer Search in development and other leadership roles.

Before he left for his next career, what Jay accomplished in those 16 years of sustained effort is legendary. Today there are seven Summer Search offices, which include three Bay Area sites in San Francisco, the North Bay, and Silicon Valley, as well as offices in Boston, Seattle, New York, and Philadelphia. There will be more. Our annual budget is $15 million and growing.

Perhaps one of Jay's biggest accomplishments was dealing directly with me. Driving out to my home one sunny afternoon, he said, "Linda, Summer Search can't become a mature organization if it stays founder-driven. You have to pass it on."

Given that I knew how much he loved me, and how much it cost him, I was never so proud of Jay as in that moment. Yet, at the same time, I was too wounded to care.

The wounds ran deeper, much deeper. My husband of 40 years had been acting increasingly strange. Something was terribly wrong. Finally, in his late sixties, he was diagnosed with possible Alzheimer's, which soon became a full-blown dementia. I wondered: he had been a superstar, an outstanding achiever since childhood. Do the brightest lights fade soonest? In the end, it didn't matter; he left me long before he died.

In spite of those hard years, it was time to flip the script. Founders do limit a program's ability to grow and change. My dream will live on because I turned Summer Search over to the talented young professionals who worked with me for many years and were eager and ready to grab the reins.

During my husband's long illness, I also began to recognize something else. Successful aging also means learning to let go. As human beings, we resist this unfamiliar challenge because we are programmed, wired, to hang on. In that decade of gradual loss, my life was choked with sorrow. Yet, at the same time, out of the void, new openings, new possibilities emerged. My adult children and grandchildren were thrilled to have me more fully present in their lives. To my intense surprise, I was able to start over. I would marry again.

As for Summer Search, it took over a year to find a new leader who had the strength, intuitive smarts, and psychological-mindedness to immediately grasp the complexity of our mission. Stanford- and Harvard-educated, Amy Saxton jumped on board to help us build on our solid foundation. In the coming decade, Summer Search will become an even greater national presence and expand to serve ever more students. Amy was big enough a person to ask me to continue part-time consulting, helping mentors understand their complicated roles and coaching those students who needed help with public speaking. I am now a lucky grandmother both in my personal and professional life!

As for my legacy? *We are making the desert bloom.*

| eleven |

Meditation: Vasny

If you can show me how to cling to that which is real to me, while teaching me a way into the larger society, then I will not only drop my defenses and my hostility, but I will sing your praises and I will help you make the desert bear fruit.

—Ralph Ellison

Letting go brings time to reflect. But where does reflection lead? For me always, always it is the same. Thirteen years ago. Mission High School. A time when everything was a miracle. A time when Katherine and I were a team, the fingers of the same hand—and the moment when we both fell in love with a neglected and discarded boy. His name was Vasny.

In reflection, the past often becomes the present. I can see it, feel it, even now: Katherine and I are midway through a stalled and increasingly tense interview. She is nervous, and I realize that I am too. I wonder why. Then I look at the tough-looking, tough-talking sophomore from Guatemala sitting in front of us. Two black eyes glare back defiantly. His hands, folded on the desk, are like my father's: scarred and calloused. His skin is gray, the color of poverty.

The silence is heavy. Before I can ask him what he is thinking, he spits out, "Why me?"

No one has ever asked us this question so directly and so angrily. I don't know how to answer. I look across at Katherine—she too is pulling a blank.

Unlike most students, he doesn't seem rattled by our silence. His intense and penetrating gaze never falters; it is we who are unsettled. He persists. "I want to know. Nobody never gave me nothing I didn't earn." I wonder, is there a trace of anguish underneath the anger and coldness? "There are kids in this school who are much smarter than me, and better, too." He leans forward with his face closer to ours, and repeats with some urgency, "So? Why me?"

His intensity makes Katherine's answer sound a little stiff. "Your vice principal recommended you, and we think that you might have the potential we look for."

"That lady don't know nothing about me neither."

That's true. Jan Hudson, the vice principal who also referred Carlton, had told us that she didn't know many facts about Vasny, but that as she watched him from her office window, hanging out, smoking on the front steps with the other Latino boys, there seemed to be something compelling about him. She couldn't really say why. She looked up his school record, and although regular attendance was a problem, his grades were pretty decent.

But right now we are about to lose him. I dart a glance at Katherine, but realize he is addressing me. Students with authority issues tend to challenge me first. I make an attempt to answer more directly. "People often ask me that question too, you know." He stares back and his eyes finally blink. "They say why are *you* doing this? And you know what? I can't answer them, because basically I don't know."

His dark eyes are such deep pools of controlled intensity that I begin to feel slightly nauseous. Is there a flicker of interest or is it my imagination? He remains silent, so I continue. "What I do know is that there are moments in life when you have a choice to play it safe or take a risk. I took a big risk when I started Summer Search. Right now, I'm offering you the chance to take that same kind of risk, expose yourself to something new."

"Do I have to let you in my shoes?"

Aha! He has heard about the interview. I merely nod. He throws one last hard look at me, glances at Katherine, and then without another word, gathers up his books and leaves, slamming the door behind him. Katherine and I sit for a few minutes without speaking, trying to understand what just happened.

The door swings open. It's him. No one speaks as he sits down and stares at me blankly for a few long seconds. Then he looks at Katherine and says, "Okay."

It's like he just agreed to bridge something unbridgeable. As Vasny opens up and starts to tell his story for the first time, it is a story we have heard too many times already. Growing up with two immigrant parents who work all the time then come home and take out the frustrations of poverty's many deprivations on each other was hard. And it was lonely. There was little time or energy for him. Finally, they divorce.

By middle school, Vasny is ready to explode, and does. He hits the streets, drinking, smoking weed, and, most of all, fighting. Even though at school he is mostly high on marijuana, he is still identified as a boy with potential. Vasny's anger began to take on new meaning. This decision to expose himself—a decision that seems to be at war with an intense need to protect his fragile dignity feels heartbreaking. And he is soulful—worried about why other kids wouldn't get this opportunity. Still questioning the order of things, the fairness of things, even when life has already been so unfair to him.

As the interview comes to a close, Katherine asks, "Why is it so scary for you to accept a scholarship?"

"It don't make no sense."

"Meaning what?"

"To take something for nothing. I don't trust nobody for doing something like that."

Katherine glances at me and I know what she is thinking.

Before she can say anything Vasny looks at her and adds, "Nobody cared." She nods for him to go on, and he says, "I know I'm smart, but I'll probably drop out. My dad wants me to work with him fulltime instead of going to school." Katherine starts to protest, and he shrugs. "It don't matter, that's just the way it is."

At age 15, Vasny already seems defeated. And like so many other kids who are prematurely locked out of mainstream society, this defeat feels relentless, crushing, and permanent. Will he ever find a way in? But then, is he even looking for one? We are going to put an opportunity in front of him. What will he do? What should we do?

When the interview finally ends, Katherine gives him a handbook and the brochure to one of our most nurturing programs, a family run wilderness expedition in Colorado called Deer Hill. After he leaves, Katherine tells me she doesn't think we will ever hear from him again. I agree.

When he calls three days later, Katherine answers. Vasny tells her, somewhat awkwardly, that he has decided to accept the scholarship. For a boy who feels that accepting something from anyone is a capitulation, this feels like a huge moment. And so this boy, Katherine, and I begin our journey together—a significant journey that will leave each one of scared and transformed.

Vasny's decision to take the unusual risk of becoming emotionally vulnerable soon begins to cause internal conflict in this compromised young man. He pulls back, has trouble following through, can't allow himself to trust. His father's low expectations, too much manual labor too soon, and the lack of opportunity to dream of something better have blunted his vision. It feels like he is unable to even imagine what he is about to do; yet, at the same time, he finds himself compelled to do it. Vasny leaves for his month away without calling to say good-bye.

When he returns, we don't give him a hard time. Besides, he calls the day he gets home. Katherine and I both get on the phone and hear him say, "I'm back!" By taking the risk of indicating that he knows we care about him Vasny immediately has to cover up this moment of weakness and reverts to his characteristic nonchalance. "It was okay."

Katherine smiles at me. We both keep quiet. Vasny pauses a beat before adding, "One thing was really weird, though. The kids in my group aren't going home like me. They were all going on to other camps. It's like they didn't have families or nothing." Katherine makes a sympathetic sound as Vasny continues, "Yeah. Like there was this girl, her parents are both doctors. She had to go to three camps over the summer. She cried about it in circle. You know, that's when we talk at night, the whole group."

"I guess that's the point of circle, Vasny," Katherine says softly. "Everyone has a story."

"Tell you the truth, I felt kinda sorry for her."

"What about you?" Katherine asks. There is a brief pause, and she and I exchange looks. Vasny still doesn't answer, so she asks, "Did you let the other group members get in your shoes?"

"At first I wasn't going to, then I did. But they didn't understand some things." All three of us pause. He says, "Stuff, you know."

"Like what?" Katherine asks with perfect timing.

"I told them that in my neighborhood I have to mug people, you know, stare at them, to keep their distance. They thought that meant stealing things. Damn! I was the only Latino there."

What to say to this? But Vasny doesn't need a response; he's already talking about his trip. "We started down the San Juan River, then hiked through some really cool canyons. Katherine, we saw the most amazing sunsets and shooting stars, then we went to live with the Navajos. I was living my dream. I kept remembering what you guys told me, that this would change my life, but I didn't believe you. Thank you for giving me this trip."

I reach over and squeeze Katherine's hand. He has changed. This closed and suspicious boy is finding a way to receive that doesn't diminish him or threaten his fragile manhood.

As Vasny talks more about the landscape and the wondrous things he saw, he is so amazingly descriptive that Katherine spontaneously asks him to speak at the Fall Event. To our mutual surprise, he readily agrees. It seems like he is always catching us off guard. Or, maybe, he is just one step ahead.

In the following weeks, Vasny calls frequently to practice his speech. Then, the afternoon before the event, he calls, sounding agitated. His father is pressuring him to drop out of high school and start working. Before Summer Search, this would have been okay. But now it is upsetting, because he has different ideas, new thoughts about himself and his future.

Katherine has an answer: "Don't worry, Vasny. As long as you move forward, you will never lose us."

"I'm not afraid that I'll lose you," he says with exasperation. "I'm afraid you'll lose me."

We don't know what to say. As if reading our minds, Vasny continues, "You know, everyone always talks about what you guys give. No one ever talks about how much you take."

He is right. The complexities of Vasny's life suddenly make our reassurances seem patronizing. We both feel an overwhelming sense of resignation. Yes, it takes a lot to change, and this boy's bravery is almost frightening. Maybe that is why Katherine and I find him so compelling. We are asking him to give up all he has to make this leap into the unknown and in spite of the risks, in spite of the costs, he is doing it. For now, Katherine only adds, "Let's take it one step at a time. We'll see you tomorrow night."

At the Fall Event, people are still settling into their seats when Vasny starts speaking without notes. Within seconds, there is a profound silence as, for the first time in his life, he demonstrates that his voice matters.

> One day at school I got a call from the vice principal's office. This lady I have never met before greets me with a smile like she knows me. She says she's seen some of my work. And she says what I've heard before, that I wasn't living up to my potential. She goes on to tell me that I might be offered a scholarship with this program called Summer Search.
>
> I look at this lady for a while, thinking of what to think. Then I get mad 'cause she is insulting me. Nobody never gave me nothing I didn't earn. She tells me to go home and think about it. I never think about it once.
>
> The next day that same vice principal calls me again and asks, "Where would you like to go if you got the chance?" I tell her that it has always been a dream of mine to go camping, to live outdoors. So that night I went home and spoke to my father. He was quiet for a while, thinking about who was going to help him in the summer. Then he says to go ahead, take the interview, and try for some kind of camping trip.
>
> My vice principal said that Linda and Katherine might make my skin crawl, but not to worry.

Vasny pauses; there's a trace of a smile on his face as he continues.

> I wasn't worried, but in that interview I got scared. A part of me wanted to get up and walk away, but another part just couldn't stop talking. I had never told anybody my feelings before.
>
> And so I went to Colorado.

The audience listens intently to Vasny's descriptions of his first experience with nature and beauty and what that triggers in him.

> At night, while looking at the shooting stars, I started going through a sort of cleansing process. Learning different ways to let out my anger, I began to feel more at ease, and sleeping at night wasn't such a struggle anymore. I started looking at aspects of my life, like cutting classes, doing bad in school, fighting everyone, and I thought it will only be a matter of time before I end up dead. At Deer Hill, for the first time in my life, I was admired for something that I did good. I was admired because I have the ability to work hard. And I taught my new friends how to work.

Vasny looked around the auditorium with his penetrating black eyes.

> Deer Hill gave me hope and the chance to dream. I have been back now for over a month, and I am proud to say that I'm doing exceptionally good in school, and the streets are no longer a part of me. I used to think that no one would give me a second chance, that nobody cared, that I was locked out. All of you have proven me wrong.

The audience almost explodes with relief and applause: relief that this unbearably honest and intense testimonial is over, and applause for Vasny's extraordinary victory.

The next day, a friend, the headmistress of a private school, calls and tells me, "I will never forget that speech, and I will never forget that boy."

"There is something else you should know," I tell her, relishing the moment, "something that reminds me that this country still works." I pause for a second then add, "Chelsea Clinton took the same trip as Vasny when she was his age."

* * *

After the Fall Event, there is a long silence. We are not surprised that he goes underground for a while. Katherine and I agree that we should let him have some space. At the same time, we know that whenever anyone drops their defenses and becomes more open, it immediately makes them more vulnerable. Katherine decides to visit him at Mission—just to connect.

Before we know it, it's January and a new interview season is starting. It is time to schedule a visit at Vasny's school, a move I have delayed because it's painful just to think about what happened at Mission. The San Francisco superintendent of schools, Waldemar Rojas, decided that test scores weren't rising fast enough, so he fired the dedicated administrators Jan and Lupe. The students walked out; the parents protested; the mayor, Willie Brown, objected. Even the local police got involved, because the upsurge in school attendance meant less loitering and trouble in the neighborhood. No matter—all the positive efforts were wiped out. The kids responded as discarded kids everywhere do: by separating into racial groups and venting their rage and frustration at each other.

As Katherine and I drive through the gated parking lot now, we feel a sense of dread. We try to steel ourselves for the inevitable changes, but nothing prepares us for what we see. The expansive hallways are again littered with a combination of garbage, paper, chewing gum, and spit. The students have been trashed, so why not do the same to the floors and walls? The tension between the hall monitors and kids is palpable. We are careful not to bump against anyone as we walk through the crowded hallway.

Eight Summer Search students are tucked away in the library, a relatively safe haven on the fourth floor, waiting for their interviews. The two new ones look frightened, and the six students already in the program seem like long-lost brothers and sisters. Finally, it is time to meet with Vasny. When he walks into the room, our hearts sink. The blank look has returned; those black eyes lack intensity, and he seems hardened. When Katherine asks him how he feels about the changes at Mission, he merely shrugs and says, "It don't matter."

This indifferent attitude surely masks the many losses in his life. Mission is just one more disappointment. Katherine and I sit quietly as Vasny gives us an update that scares us. Throughout the fall he has worked in construction jobs with his father until late in the night. Then he sleeps through classes, even misses entire days of school; it seems more inevitable than ever that he will become a high school dropout.

Vasny can't look us in the eye as he adds that just one week ago, with no warning, his father threw $10 in his face and took off for Guatemala, leaving him completely without resources. He can live with his mother, but he will have to pay for room and board. It's time to quit school. "What difference does it make?" He glances at Katherine defiantly. "No one ever finishes high school in my family anyway."

"What about Summer Search helping you find a part-time job?" Katherine asked.

"I'm not disabled!"

"No, you aren't disabled, yet." I interrupt. "Listen carefully, Vasny. Think of your life as a boxing ring, and you as the boxer. Your goal is to stay in the center of the ring. There you have movement, flexibility, choices. Dropping out of high school will put you in the corner, and frankly, a corner you probably will never get out of." He stares at me blankly until I begin to feel uneasy. "Do you hear me?" I ask.

His gaze drops and he puts his head in his hands. I wait, until I see a slight nod, so I continue: "Before you make a final decision, there's something else you should think about." Vasny slowly raises his head and stares at me.

"We have another scholarship. This time, it's with an amazing program called Where There Be Dragons. Call us crazy, but Katherine and I believe that you have a spiritual side. That you care about people and that side needs to be recognized and nourished so you can bring that spirit to your community." Vasny looks at me like I am indeed crazy. As I catch Katherine's raised eyebrow, it occurs to me that maybe he is right. I push on doggedly. "This program has a scholarship for one Summer Search student to go to Nepal this summer."

Vasny's hooded eyes are dark and unreadable. He doesn't answer, so I tell him more about this unique program, which involves trekking and community service. It is the trip of a lifetime, but it's his call. I also remind him that, if we continue to invest in him, he will have to start investing in himself and his education. He leaves without responding. On the way back to the office, Katherine warily questions this risky decision and what it might mean to Vasny and to us.

He calls a few days later and tells Katherine he has decided to go. There are practical things that need to be done immediately. He has to support himself, but has no money. There is a part-time job opening posted near our office at a deli, but transportation is a problem. There are buses, but it will take two precious hours to get there, a four-hour round-trip every day—time Vasny doesn't have if he goes to school regularly. By some twist of fate, a donor has just offered to donate his older car to Summer Search. Vasny has gotten his license, so we make the unusual and highly questionable decision to loan him this car for the next three months.

Two months later, Vasny calls to tell us he has had an accident. No one is seriously hurt, but the car is totaled—a good lesson about crossing a line with a student, something we never should have done.

It got him through a temporary crisis, but clearly we took on too much responsibility.

Right now he needs to pick up his stuff from the car at the junk yard in South San Francisco, and we need to get the pink slip. Katherine is at a school in Oakland, so I decide to go. It is an uncharacteristically hot day in Marin, so I only bring a light sweater as I head into the city. By the time I drive across the Golden Gate Bridge, cold fog is starting to pour in.

I meet Vasny at Mission High, and we head down to South San Francisco for what is going to be a very long wait for a smashed car. We don't talk much. My teeth are chattering from the cold, and his heart seems closed. Anyway, what is there to say? We sit in silence.

Finally, the car is pulled forward by a tractor. We retrieve Vasny's things, and I get the pink slip. Then I drive him back to school for an evening meeting. As the car stops, I sit for a minute. Then I turn to give him a hug. It takes a few seconds for him to hug me back. When he does he whispers, "Linda, I'm sorry, so sorry."

In spite of all the things inside me screaming, *How could you?* I only say, "Vasny, it doesn't matter—all that really matters is that you are okay."

* * *

That summer, the director of Where There Be Dragons phones to tell us that there is trouble on the Nepal trip. A student with severe diarrhea and dehydration has to be evacuated by helicopter, leaving the group with just one leader for two days. Normally that would be okay, but three of the kids are real troublemakers. There is also a rumor that they are smoking marijuana, a serious offense. If they are caught, they will be sent home. I wonder how those problems are affecting Vasny.

As the other Summer Search kids check in during the fall, we hear stories, stories, and then more stories. The adolescent brain is wired for impulsive actions and risk-taking. For boys, the need to be heroic is palpable, yet there are few ways to engage in positive risk-taking. As they call in, almost all of the boys talk proudly about their exploits: catching another student falling down a precipice or rescuing one of their group members from threatening rapids. In short, saving a life. We comment on their strength and power, and we listen to them chuckle as they shyly admit that, yes, it was hard, but it's true: they had been very brave!

For many of the young women, the risk-taking takes a different form. Their sense of fulfillment seems to come from becoming more emotionally vulnerable by daring to create more authentic relationships. Katherine and I speculate. Why are girls so often forced to close off so much of their inner richness at home and at school?

As we talk about those differences, we brag about the kids we have mentored and revel in their huge successes. For each of us, the underlying feeling is also one of relief. The long summer of responsibility is finally over. Almost. One last person has yet to check in. Late one afternoon, I am alone in the office when Vasny finally calls. His voice is neutral as he says, "It was a good trip. Quite an experience."

"Tell me about it!"

"Well, it was the trip of a lifetime. How about that?"

"Come on, Vasny!" I wonder if his coolness means he has gotten into trouble. "Were there any problems?" He doesn't answer, so I say, "I heard there was a helicopter evacuation." There is another brief silence. "How about the marijuana?" I ask.

"They were so rich, they could get away with anything!" Vasny stumbles for the right words before continuing. "They...they bathed in money!" He pauses again, "I'm not going to lie to you, I did smoke. It was in your face all of the time, but I was responsible. Three of the kids were wasted."

"What do you mean?"

"They were wasted. They talked and acted like trash. Like there was this day in a small town called Pokhara. That afternoon, the girls went off with the female leader. Us guys were alone because the other leader took the sick kid off by helicopter. Anyway, we rowed out to this place in the middle of a lake. They started to drink beers. I don't drink anymore, so I told them, 'I don't want to be the babysitter.' But they kept drinking. It was getting dark and starting to rain, and we had to get back across the lake. This one guy, Clark, got really drunk and started trying to pick a fight. Jeff, another rich guy—he was cool, though—helped me keep him in the boat. Clark kept trying to fight. I kept telling him to stop it. You see, I've almost drowned twice, and I'm really afraid of water."

He pauses.

"What happened?"

"I finally got them back to solid ground. Then I got a taxi to take them back to the hotel. Clark still wanted to fight, and then he and the other one started talking trash again. They started shouting out the taxi window, 'Where are the girls? Take us to the girls!' I was embarrassed, Linda. They were just young boys, and they were stupid drunk, but the Nepalese people are so gentle. There aren't even any swear words in their language."

"The ugly American, huh?" How strange that a tough kid from the worst area of the inner city had taken on the role of leader and role model to teenagers from the most privileged families. "I'm so proud of you for the way you helped the group," I say.

"With God's help, I might become somebody," he responds with uncharacteristic pride. Is this the boy who saw himself as worthless?

He is not only thinking different thoughts but seems less frightened by that fact.

I'm quick to take this rare opening. "If you want to go forward, you must treat yourself better, Vasny. Next year, if you do well in school, you can get a full scholarship to boarding school for a fifth year of high school. That will give you the academic skills you didn't get at Mission. Just think about how it will feel to be around people who love books and ideas." I can tell I am getting carried away, but it seems like he is listening. "After that, you can get a full scholarship for college!"

"I'm not used to thinking like that. I can't."

"But you can."

There is a pause, then a different and dreamy voice continues: "In Nepal, Linda, I trekked through mountains and saw things I couldn't believe. My family home stay was great. I loved my host grandmother. She was so cool. The Nepalese people have very little, yet they are so genuine and happy. Our community service project was cool too. Do you know that because of us a whole village has water for the first time! When you come to Mission, I'll show you and Katherine the pictures."

There is another pregnant pause. I start to say something, but I can feel that he wants this space. This moment is his, and my silence is no longer threatening, but validating. "On this trip I had a lot of time to think," Vasny continues peacefully. "I realized it could be dangerous to become self-absorbed like some of the kids in my group, so I began to question things. One day it struck me. I am going to make a difference in this world. Right then, as I walked on foreign soil, I felt the purpose of it all." He continues, so softly that I can barely hear him. "I discovered the meaning of my life in a country as foreign as I once thought my feelings were."

Why me? The pain in his tortured, black eyes as he asked that question two years before reminds me again of the vast terrain we have covered.

Vasny, who seems to read my thoughts, adds, "I kept asking myself why? Why was I chosen? The people I know here will never get the chance to experience what I was seeing and feeling."

I am silent. Waiting. "Then, you know what? The answer just came, like the wind blowing in my face, and the river racing through my soul. One day, looking out over the mountains, it just came." The silence now feels like silk. "Linda, I want to be a teacher. This experience, this gift will be for the students who won't ever see that place or have that moment where I suspended time. I said to myself, 'Let it be for them.'"

There is a catch in my throat as I say, "Maybe you have finally found your answer." There is an intense but satisfying pause as we both try to digest what just happened. Without warning, he flips back into neutral. "Cool," he replies.

"Very cool."

"Hey, do you think I should call my essay, 'Let It Be for Them'?"

* * *

Although Vasny's living situation continues to be unstable, he starts his senior year at school with new energy. He doesn't call for a month. Then, late one night, he leaves a message that he has completed his application to Northfield Mt. Hermon for that fifth year of high school. He adds that his father has come home from Guatemala, information that makes Katherine and I uneasy.

He calls just a few days later. "I'm not going to that school, or college neither," Vasny says in a haunted voice. "I need to help out my dad."

It is late in the evening. I tell myself: *Think clearly*. Control is a critical issue. Vasny's father is pressuring him to drop out of school, which makes him feel he has no control. I don't want to add to that pressure. I answer carefully. "The important thing to remember is that we support you no matter what you do. Do you hear me?" Silence again. "But you sound terrible. What's going on?"

"I'm afraid of disappointing you and Katherine."

"That's good. I like that."

He laughs. The tension lessons a bit, and it feels okay for me to continue. "Vasny, part of being a senior in high school is changing your mind every day. Remember, your only goal right now is to stay in the center of the ring, which means don't make decisions, create choices." I hesitate. "If it's all right with you, I want to go ahead and write a letter of recommendation to Northfield."

"Okay," he says reluctantly.

Before starting that letter, I ask Katherine. Is it fair to propel Vasny so far, only to have him return to such severe limitations? We are both unsure, but I push this worry aside and write a lengthy letter about his potential and unique spirit given the challenges in his life. I also include a description of his destructive relationship with his father. As always with letters of recommendation, I sent a copy to him.

The next month, it is time to return to Mission High. Given the increasingly dire situation at the school, there are just a few new students, so Katherine doesn't come with me. Vasny is a no-show for his appointment, which makes it hard for me to concentrate. Just as I am tiredly packing up at the end of a long and discouraging morning, I see him through the glass window.

He looks worried as he hurries across the large library toward the interview room. "Where's Katherine?"

"At another school, Vasny—there are not many new students here now. What happened?"

"Didn't they tell you? I had a peer resource meeting."

Before I can tell him I'm late and have to get back to the office, he sits down and says, "I talked to my pop: so I asked him, 'Why is it so funny to you when people say I'm smart?'" Vasny stares at me and continues. "'And, Pops, why is it that all those other people are trying to help me, but you don't care?'"

"How did he react?"

Vasny continues seeming not to hear me. "I said to him, 'Why is it a joke to you that I want to go to college? It's not like it was for you growing up, Pops. I can't work like you did in the fields.'" Vasny's eyes start to fill with tears, and he struggles to control emotions that he doesn't want to feel. "Pops said it wasn't true that he puts me down," he continues. "Then he changed the subject."

I sit still as stone. Vasny's gray skin is now flushed as he bursts out, "'Why, Pops? Why? Why do you always talk about my little brother?'" In a voice that is almost a wail, "I said to him, 'Pops! Pops, what about me?'"

Vasny's eyes are no longer blank, but he doesn't look away as he now lets himself feel things he has never allowed himself to feel. With his arm, he swipes the tears. I touch his hand. "You know that I love him," he adds quietly.

"I know." A thought makes me immediately uneasy. "Did you get that letter of recommendation?"

"Yeah, but Pops saw it first. He don't read too good." Vasny looks down at the floor before continuing. "But he understood what it said, so I figured I had to talk to him."

A wave of concern makes my stomach jump. "Was it all right?"

He looks up at me for several long seconds. "Yeah. It was all right."

As Vasny tries to get back in control of his emotions, it occurs to me that it wasn't until I was in my thirties that I confronted my father. I touch his hand again. "Vasny, you could never go forward, never become free, until you had that conversation with your father. Do you know that?"

Vasny looks away and slips something else in so quickly that I almost don't catch it: "He bought me a computer."

"Really! That's amazing." For some reason I will never understand, I say, "You know, lately I've been thinking about your father. Do you think that, maybe, he's trying to tell you something?"

There is a gap between us that I can't read. When Vasny doesn't answer, I say, "He was the one to say, go ahead, try Deer Hill. By buying you a computer, do you think that he is trying, in his own way, to tell you it's okay to go to Northfield Mt. Hermon?"

Another long pause, but this one feels different. Something is wrong. There is a tearing sound as Vasny says, "Linda, you have to listen to me, and you have to tell Katherine." I look at him; the words I want to say stick in my throat. He stands up, then sits down again. "I can't."

I want to stop what is happening. There is so much more. He could have gone so far. This realization, and all that is going to be lost, brings an almost physical wave of regret.

Vasny mumbles, "Right now, I can't leave him. You have to let me go." He gives me a long look and a quick hug. "Will you tell Katherine I said good-bye?" And before I can stop him, he's gone.

I sit alone staring at the washed-out gray walls. What have I missed? What do I say to Katherine? Then Vasny's penetrating gaze comes back to me—demanding that I look beyond my own needs, toward some larger truth. This is not about the results I want. Katherine and I have overstepped. In working with any student, our role is to open doors, create possibilities, not outcomes. This isn't about losing—it is about letting go. In my haste to get to the "right" result, I forgot the process. A hardened boy, discarded so easily, has learned that he is valuable. He has also been able to confront his father. That is what has met his needs, and that has to be enough.

Yet it wasn't quite over. Even after Northfield doesn't work out, Katherine and I can't let go. We begin to push Vasny to enroll at SF City College. Perhaps in retaliation, he leaves high school, one credit short of graduating. He sends a letter to Katherine, and a different one to me, begging us to understand and accept his need to cut himself off from us and from Summer Search and to return to Guatemala.

We do not hear from him for six years.

Then, very late one night, I am working on emails, and a new message pops up. My God, it's Vasny! I sit, staring at his name in the inbox, reading it over and over before opening it. He is not only alive, but he is keeping up with Summer Search on our website. What happened to Katherine? he wants to know. I email him back that she is, of course, still with Summer Search, but she is married and has a different name. I tell him, "Vasny, we are so glad to hear from you and we think of you often. We are glad, so glad you reached out."

* * *

It is 2009, two years later. We have many new hires in seven different offices and new methods of teaching young and inexperienced staff. Katherine and I meet at the office to drive together to yet another Spring Event at Mission High, this time surrounded by new leadership and staff. We park. I see a hauntingly familiar face in the car next to us, a man with coal-black eyes. That image gets lost as we get out of the car and tons of students and alumni come running, surrounding us. It is a thrilling moment, so many kids moving forward, so much success to report!

Then, as we enter the school, standing with Jan Hudson, now a retired vice principal from Mission High, is Vasny.

Katherine and I run over with outstretched arms, which simultaneously pleases and embarrasses him. Vasny tells us he is running a telecommunications business with his father. Their company provides services all over Guatemala and Honduras. He looks at me and says shyly, "We have a fleet of over 50 trucks. The roads are very dangerous. When my drivers have accidents, I don't know why, I never blame them. I just say to them, 'Are you all right?'"

There is just a whisper of a smile on his face as he continues. He lives in Guatemala City, and he is thinking of running for political office. He is married and has a daughter. "Would you like to see her picture?" Before we can answer, he pulls out a photo of a two-year-old girl. Vasny's same coal-black eyes stare back at us. He looks at Katherine and then at me and says, "Her name is Calinda Katherine."

A childlike emotion, something I can't define, wells up inside me. Tears sting my eyes. Then, like a whisper, like a gift, it comes. A passage I remember from somewhere long ago comes to mind and makes sense for the first time: *If you bring forth what is within you, what you bring forth will save you. If you do not bring forth what is within you, what you do not bring forth will destroy you.* I look at Vasny and then at Katherine. This boy, forever changed, is now a man giving back to the world.

Letting go. I often reflect on the students I have mentored and loved over the past 25 years, on the young staff so eager to learn, on the board members and donors so personally fulfilled by their close relationships with students, on the volunteer teachers so elated as they see students from impossible backgrounds like Vasny succeeding. I think of Vasny telling me the answer just came to him like the wind blowing in his face and the river racing through his soul and I think of the thousands yet to come.

Now, on quiet, early morning runs, I pause and allow that same wind to caress my face. It is then that I finally know. For each one of us, our full measure of success in life will always and forever be the sum of what we give away.

Let it be for them.

No Man Is an Island
by Sasha Kovriga

2014. I am sitting in one of the most beautiful places in the world: San Francisco, California, where the blue of the sky hits the velvety green of the distant mountains. I can hear my daughters playing close by. I am here. I am complete. I am me.

1990. I am sitting at a table in our small one-bedroom apartment about to dial a number. Late afternoon sun peeks through the shades. It is almost spring. I am almost 17. I'd spent years dreaming of coming to America. America! The land of plenty, the land of unlimited possibilities and happy outcomes…except it doesn't feel that way. Actually, it's all very predictable. I am an outsider, a teenage one at that. My mother speaks no English and, at the age of 46, has limited employment prospects. We're receiving AFDC, a type of welfare assistance.

Yet, at my new high school, I am surrounded by kids from the wealthy suburban families—all so polished, capable, going places. They can express themselves, they have friends and lunch money and college plans. I don't.

If a clod is washed into the sea, Europe is the less. When you're poor, depressed, and a foreigner, you become one with your circumstance. The "I" starts to disappear. It becomes about surviving and pretending. The self is to be hidden, obliterated because if there is no self, you can't be depressed, lonely, or hurt. A few months prior, I tried to kill myself (a hack job—a few Tylenols are hardly lethal even to a depressed teenager). This wasn't an act of desperation but a logical move. If the whole point is to get rid of the self, why not take the ultimate step?

The call I am about to make is to this woman. The Jewish Family and Children's Service Agency had told me she might be offering a trip of some sort. Some unseen force is moving me to pick up the receiver. I am incredibly self-conscious about my English; I hate speaking on the telephone and hate speaking to strangers, and this one is an American to boot. Everything inside of me should be rebelling. Yet somehow I feel very calm. I pick up the phone. I dial. She picks up.

We talk about *me*. There are long pauses. She makes a space and then she waits. Somehow in my shriveled and depressed self, I find the courage to step into that space—to expose myself, to make myself vulnerable. I later reflect that this is the essence of love: to make yourself vulnerable and yet be accepted. Although I don't have the words to express it, I feel something very powerful. Toward the end of the call, she tells me about a biking trip in the Northwest; then she says, "Oh, yes, and there is also a trip to Israel." I say that I don't want to go to the Northwest. I want to go to Israel. In hindsight, this seems so minor. But at the time, the ability to say no and to acknowledge what *I* wanted, was momentous. After only 45 minutes, the "I" was beginning to reappear. The journey back to me had begun.

Twenty-four years have passed since that moment, the importance of which has only grown stronger in retrospect. There was an adult, a stranger who seemed to care for *me*. Not some invented self, but *me* as I was; with all my weakness and sadness. "There must be something valuable, something special about *me*, even as the rest of the world seemed to convey the opposite," I concluded, if only subconsciously. "And since I am valuable, I am not powerless, I can do things. I can break free of my limitations even if I don't quite yet know how!" All of this in 45 minutes. If this isn't magic, I don't know what is.

That interview was not the end but the beginning of the journey. The sense of self-worth that budded in that moment was very fragile indeed; the sense of agency, of power to direct and impact my own destiny, was only a sapling. I needed more tending and support.

And so came the trip to Israel, where I became a full-fledged member of the group, the person who was liked, respected, and perhaps most importantly, relied upon. I was not some little Soviet immigrant who could do nothing and was going nowhere; I was one of them—these fabulous, successful, and good-looking American teenagers. While my judgment about the merits of my peers was probably exaggerated, just like my judgment about the lack of merit in myself was overblown, the empowerment that I got from being a member of my group was transformational. I was turning into a new person—a person who was facing the world instead of hiding from it.

As I returned home armed with this new expanded view and in the early stages of forging a new identity, the world I was familiar with had remained the same—full of limitations and hopelessness. It was at that point that I was at my most fragile. And so the ongoing relationship with *her*, my mentor, took on even more importance. She encouraged me to write an essay reflecting on my trip. The act of writing down my experiences was in itself incredibly important. Once committed to paper, there was no turning back from my new self.

As I look back over what happened next, I have a lot to be proud of. I graduated from a university with top honors, got a master's degree in philosophy, worked for a top consulting firm, and graduated with an MBA from Harvard Business School. Currently I am a portfolio manager and a partner at a respected money management firm in San Francisco. I have three lovely daughters and a beautiful wife. I am a member of several nonprofit boards and active in the philanthropic community.

Yet that's not the whole story. Without fully understanding it, I made a Faustian bargain. Summer Search opened the door to a world of opportunities and possibilities; it helped me develop the skills to navigate that new world and seemingly didn't ask for anything in return.

So not true! Summer Search burdened me with the gift of insight about myself. While I am ultimately responsible for my own life… *no man is an island.* To the extent that we become successful, we owe a debt of gratitude to the people who were willing to help us on our way. For most kids, these people are their family and their community. For Summer Search kids, these people are complete strangers.

I have benefited from *her*, she who gave up her comfortable life to spend 12-hour days to mentor students such as myself and remains committed year after year to their success. There are now 157 listening mentors like *her* and thousands of students like *me* in seven different offices nationwide. And we have benefited from the willingness of hundreds of other people who have never met us as they gave of themselves and their financial resources to ensure our success. And those numbers are growing.

The concept of the "circle of moral concern" comes into play here. For many people, this circle includes only themselves, maybe their family. For others it's a bit bigger—it includes their community. And for some, the lucky few, the circle extends to the "other."

And so, 24 years later, I understand and live the true import of my Summer Search experience through the desire and the power to not only enlarge my own life but the burning need to expand my circle of moral concern to change the lives of the "other." *Therefore never send to know for whom the bell tolls; it tolls for thee.*

Affection motivates us to see everything about another. Empathy opens us to absorb the good and the bad. Love impels us not to just observe but to think as another thinks and to feel as another feels.

—David Brooks, on the best way to investigate social problems

Acknowledgments

It is impossible to even begin to adequately thank the many people who have supported Summer Search over the past 25 years. On reflection, I am grateful that I created something that has transcended me and successfully transferred to others who have become as passionately engaged. Those individuals, including the staff we train, the teachers who identify students, and the donors who fund the program, are deeply committed and love Summer Search and the kids with a ferocity that is astounding. I send my love and gratitude in return. There are too many of you to be mentioned but I know and you know who you are.

I want to thank specific individuals who played a role in the creation of this amazing program but it is a tall order. First, the people who stepped forth when Summer Search was a new and vulnerable idea. There was Jim Klingbeil, a businessman who I didn't know very well, who told me to stop talking and "get off my ass and do something." Two prominent people in the philanthropic community, John Osterweis and Sally Hambrecht, to my great surprise, agreed to join the newly formed board of directors. John would serve as president for the next 14 years, providing steady leadership as the little idea twisted and turned and expanded into the life-changing force it is today. Sally's dramatic role in the program is explained in the chapter about Solaria.

Early donors who took me seriously as I stumbled through presentations were John Lee, Susan Blake, and Linda Gruber. As I think of each one of you it brings tears to my eyes. And then there was the late Meg Quigley and her partner, Judi Hiltner. Meg loved Mills College and Summer Search. She brought the two together through a significant donation to Mills College for scholarships targeted for qualified Summer Search young women. Another important person was Barney Osher, who nearly scared me to death at an early luncheon. The Bernard Osher Foundation went on to become a major force in the program by providing an annual fund for emergency and enrichment opportunities for our college students who had the courage to fly high but were without safety nets.

Jay Jacobs and Katherine Kennedy are mentioned in this book but more needs to be said. The sheer luck of both of them emerging at year five and becoming the first hires and soon leaders provided the path for all the others to follow. It keeps amazing me. Jay opened our first satellite office in Boston along with board chair Fredi Stevenson and then moved on to develop Summer Search into a national program. Katherine has dedicated her professional career to Summer Search. Today she is a steady presence and loving role model in the lives of our alumni as well as a wise counsel for an ever growing staff.

Three other young staff members who need special recognition are Eden Werring, Emily Edwards, and Jessica Vibberts. Eden came to us fresh out of Yale and immediately brought a keen intelligence to the developing mentoring model. She went on to start and successfully lead our North Bay and then opened our New York office with the support of the first board chair. Emily, also fresh out of college, helped Jay develop the Boston office and went on at a very early age to become Executive Director. Today she continues to remind us of what personal excellence looks like as she plays a major role in the national expansion effort. Jessica, on staff at the North Bay office, became the Executive Director after a short period. During a time of intense change Jessica stepped up to become our national interim leader, and that leadership has helped us to maintain our culture and deeply felt values as we continue to innovate. I must add that each of these individuals has played a heroic role as they read and reread my manuscript over the years! Finally, I am intensely grateful to our current national leader, Amy Saxton, a woman of great intellect and passion for the work and a phenomenal person to lead the national expansion to double and triple the number of students we serve.

Three other significant individuals to offer their love and resources to Summer Search are Dana Emery, Ted Williams, and Bob Friend. Dana got involved early on as a board member through the Junior League. She valiantly tried to help me become more organized and suggested we have committees—a great idea! Dana was the first president of our national board and raised the bar to a whole new level. (Including committees.) Ted Williams has loved this program for more than 15 years and is currently an enormously effective president of the national board. And Bob Friend—what can be said about a man who cries at events, who cries at the students' stories, who brings a heart as big as the universe? If there is one heart that beats for all of us in Summer Search, it is the heart of Bob Friend.

Then there was the power of unexpected generosity from random people. In the beginning it was John Moriarity, a man who happened to read a story in the newspaper about one of my students. He was sponsoring more than 30 students on his own to give them access to college. It was John who introduced me to the teachers who would change Summer Search. John was followed by David Wilson, a man who runs his own family foundation. He came to my office for a 15-minute site visit and stayed for the next 20 years. David continues to expertly mentor the emerging leadership in Summer Search with persistence and patience. In those early days I had the privilege of meeting Carol Tolan, a woman whose passion for social justice and astute intellect provided me the mentoring that I cherish to this day.

About those teachers—there have been hundreds already and growing numbers of these generous people who volunteer their precious time and energy to nominate students. In the early days in San Francisco there were the dynamic four: Georganne Ferrier, Jan Hudson, Lettie Lupus, and Florence O'Malley, career teachers who dropped everything to work with me and then to follow and support their students as their lives began to change. There is one day I will never forget. Florence, the dean of students, and I were walking toward the interview room. As she was explaining about the mouth-watering lunch she had prepared, including her signature brownies, a student in front of us down the long hall pushed another student to the floor. Florence shouted but he paid no attention, at which point she took off her shoe and threw it, getting his full attention.

The students—those brave, brave students who applied to a program they barely understood and who put up with my badgering as they struggled with the huge challenges they faced (as we all do) when confronted with the opportunities as well as the dangers of transformation. I continue to admire and love these students as they now are becoming generous leaders and role models for others.

The proudest achievement of my life is my family. I started Summer Search in 1990 when my last daughter went off to college. Neither my husband, Pierre, nor myself had the slightest comprehension of what was about to happen. We truly did not see it coming. When it blossomed, he was so proud of me. What Pierre didn't fully realize was that I was channeling him and all that I had learned from him in our long marriage. Before developing dementia in his midsixties Pierre was the most outstanding therapist and wisest student of human nature I have ever known. His voice is in every part of this book.

As my beloved three children, Sascha, Sara, and Mara, and their spouses, Mimi and Eric, watched me dedicate the last two decades of my life to impact those so much less fortunate, I have the extreme privilege today of watching them develop their own philanthropic interests. As a family, in our different ways, we all share the value of leveling the playing field and find the same sense of purpose and joy in our efforts.

Over the years many people have read and offered advice on the manuscript. Almost always it triggered growth. There were three amazing people I would like to especially recognize. Miranda Popkey, an editor who responded to my submission with a rejection but also pages of notes and observations. All incredibly astute and helpful. Editors like foundation officers can have so much more to offer than money or acceptance or rejection. A complete stranger, Harold Davis, in one phone call asked me to send the entire manuscript which he read that afternoon. His feedback dramatically altered the tone of the book and I am forever grateful. And then there was Eden Weering, whose brilliant eye for detail and fine writing nearly drove me over the edge but whose love and contribution is in every page.

I cannot end without mentioning my agent, who has become a family member as well. Priscilla Regan, of Olive Branch Agency, is an 80-year-old expert in judging writing, judging people, and judging promise. She jumped on the bandwagon and got this book a wonderful publisher. But, most importantly, she taught me to believe that I was a writer. As a farm girl and student nurse from Indiana who came to California on a Greyhound bus, the road to finding my own voice was long. When, almost accidentally, I created a program that would change the trajectory of thousands of young people, I developed a new kind of confidence—but never as a writer. Over the three-year process of producing this book, after each rejection Priscilla was right there to emphasize what I was learning—how to become a better writer. With her mentoring and skill building I have finally become much closer to what I have aspired to be for so long— the writer who could make these stories and this book the best it could be.

To conclude, for the reader who has persisted through the book to this final point, thank you. If you are interested in a video of a speech by a Summer Search student I suggest you check into a speech by Carlos Romero given at an event well over a decade ago it is the speech that keeps on giving. https://www.summersearch.org/carlos-romero